THEY SHOOT MANAGERS, DON'T THEY?

MANAGING YOURSELF AND LEADING
OTHERS IN A CHANGING WORLD

They Shoot Managers, Don't They?

by Terry L. Paulson, Ph.D.

TEN SPEED PRESS
Berkeley, California

1⊜

TEN SPEED PRESS
P. O. Box 7123
Berkeley, California 94707

First Printing 1991

Cover Design by Fifth Street Design
Text design and typography by Hal Hershey

Libary of Congress Cataloging-in-Publication Data
Paulson, Terry L.
    They shoot managers, don't they? : making conflict work in a changing world
    / Terry L. Paulson.
            p.   cm.
    Includes bibliographical references.
    ISBN 0-89815-429-4 :
    1. Conflict management. 2. Industrial management. 3. Psychology, Industrial.
    4. Organizational behavior. I. Title.
    HD42.P38 1991   658.4—dc20   91-12200
                                                                         CIP

Printed in the United States of America

    3   4   5   —   95   94   93

To my beloved mother and father, Ann and Homer Paulson,
who in their special way made me realize anything
was possible with faith in God and a sense of humor.

To my son Sean
who has made me grow up
at least a step ahead of him.

And finally, to my wife, Lorie
whose positiveness and ready smile have proved
to be my greatest source of encouragement.

Acknowledgements

This book has been in the process of becoming for years. Its completion is a result of the support and prodding of many colleagues. But it would never have been finished without the practical input and sobering feedback from thousands of managers I have worked with as a trainer and professional speaker. They demanded programs that were practical, down-to-earth, and entertaining. I have tried to carry that same winning balance into this book.

A special acknowledgement goes to Mark Falstein whose skill as a writer and quick study habits as an editor helped take my audiotapes, articles, and half-finished rough drafts and shape them into a concise and readable manuscript. He worked hard to tighten content without sacrificing my style or my humor. I am satisfied that he succeeded. As a result, any problems you find in this book belong to me. I am thankful that Mark was there to make any such shortcomings less obvious.

Sharon Riding, my administrative assistant at Paulson & Associates Inc., has always been an inspiration to me. Her dedicated work ethic, warmth, and lasting friendship have been major factors in the completion of this book. In the face of my hectic speaking responsibilities, she kept the business wheels spinning smoothly while I wrote.

I want to thank Lee and Marlene Canter and their fine staff at Lee Canter & Associates for believing enough in the book to publish it. A special appreciation goes to Phil Wood and the dedicated staff at Ten Speed Press. They have provided the direction and the support to give this book the special treatment and the attention it deserves.

I've already dedicated the book to my family. They are a special family, and provide the base of support, vitality, and values that make you want to achieve for them. For what you have given me in the past and what you continue to give on into the future, I thank you.

Finally, to all those managers and customers who kept asking me to write a book, thank you. There would have been no book without your persistent questioning, your input, and patronage.

Contents

Don't Get Your Bags Sent to Japan Unless You're Going There

"Before you start on the road of revenge, dig two graves."
—Chinese proverb

Not long ago I was flying to Los Angeles, where I was scheduled to speak at a conference. I was at Kennedy Airport in New York, standing in line to check my bags, and the guy in front of me was giving the baggage checker a difficult time. He was being terribly, obnoxiously abusive. I didn't say anything—the man was not only upset, he was big. After he moved away from the curb, I expressed my sympathy to the checker for the verbal bullying he had taken.

"Do people talk that way to you often?" I asked him.

"Oh, yeah. You get used to it around here."

"Well, I don't think I'd get used to it."

"Don't worry, bud," he drawled, as he slapped the tags on my suitcases. "After all, the customer's always right."

I'm a psychologist; I had a pretty good idea he didn't really mean that. "Well, I don't think he was right in this case," I said.

"Don't worry," the checker repeated with quiet confidence, swinging my bags onto the conveyor belt behind him. "I've already gotten even."

"What do you mean?" I said, my eyes opening wide in growing concern.

"He's on his way to Chicago," the man said, "but his bags are going to Japan."

I laughed—I don't think I'd ever been more friendly to an individual in my entire life. I wanted to go to L.A., and I wanted my bags to go there with me. They did, but over the next few days, I kept thinking about the incident and the valuable truth it so eloquently taught. Unless you have the ability to manage conflict successfully, your actions or inactions can allow it to escalate into guerilla warfare. Some people don't get mad; they just get even. You can be one hundred-percent right and still have your bags sent to Japan.

Reprinted by permission of United Feature Syndicate, Inc.

This is a book about managing yourself and leading others in a changing world. It's also about the conflict generated and the way we handle it, or, to be more precise, the way we usually don't handle it. Most of us are either intimidated into avoiding conflict entirely (the Charlie Brown solution) or else feel pressured into coming on like the corporate version of Attila the Hun. Both are ineffective. The trick is to find that elusive middle ground somewhere between doormat and steamroller.

The ability to deal with change and conflict as a manager is vital, whether you're a corporate executive caught in a jurisdictional border war with an ambitious colleague, a school administrator burdened with a troublesome and marginally competent teacher, or even a parent trying to handle a difficult teenager. (*Especially* if you're trying to handle a difficult teenager.)

> *"I am convinced that if the rate of change inside an organization is less than the rate of change outside, the end is in sight."*
>
> **—John Welch, CEO of GE**

In this time of rapid change, conflict is built into the very fabric of most of our companies and civic institutions. Rarely do you hear any talk these days about conflict resolution; it's conflict management now. If you've ever felt that some people in your organization were put there for the express purpose of frustrating you, it's probably true. Do they really shoot managers? Not legally, but it sure feels that way for managers caught in the middle of change. Checks and balances are built in to maintain the tensions between change and the status quo, between cost containment and revenue expansion, between being creative and losing focus. Conflict can sap the morale of an organization, or it can be an asset. Properly managed, it can help set the stage for challenge and change. It can inspire creativity, raise alternative solutions, redirect efforts, clarify goals and expectations, and eliminate unnecessary work. It can energize and motivate people, provide them with a more positive group identity, and increase trust within an organization. In short, positively directed conflict can work for you in a changing world.

> *"The achievement of excellence can occur only if the organization promotes a culture of creative dissatisfaction."*
> —Lawrence Miller

But unless you can manage conflict successfully, you're in a no-win situation, even if it may for a time feel like you've won. No doubt that guy flying to Chicago felt like a winner all the way up to the baggage claim area at O'Hare Airport. He had every right to want to get to Chicago as fast as he could, but he forgot how important it is to keep the right people working to make it happen.

Consider the following cases. Do any of these situations sound familiar?

The across-the-board cutbacks at B.B. Bunzner Electronics were designed to create a tighter ship to weather the strong new competition from the Far East. For Chip Fardling, the vice president of engineering, what they mainly created was a headache. According to the CEO, what was needed was excellence, creativity, cost-containment, and productivity, and it needed to start yesterday. Two of Chip's top engineers had succumbed to the pressure; they had left for lucrative salaries and better working conditions elsewhere. The gaping holes in their projects had put new-product design schedules on the rocks. Chip tried to confront his boss with the problems and with his need for many more hands to get the department back on course. The CEO's short lecture was far from inspiring: "You heard the boss! No new people! You've been over-staffed for years! If you're not up to the task, we'll get someone in who is!" At a time when people needed to pull together, everyone was more interested in covering up the problems than dealing with them. Many were sending out their resumes and hanging on until they could find new positions. Chip decided to play the same game.

*   *   *   *   *   *

Jan Jekyll was an experienced administrator at East Fishgill Community College. When she accepted a position as dean of philosophy at the prestigious University of California at Santa Clausa, she was not prepared for the resistance she received from Frederic Fixture, one of the tenured professors. She was appalled by his weak, outdated curriculum and his lackluster class performance; and his participation in department meetings had been less than constructive. She confronted him privately and was shocked by his response. "Listen, honey," he said, lurching around and brandishing his cigarette at her. "Back off! I've been tenured here for thirteen years and I'll be here long after you leave. You can't touch me, so get off my back!" Two and a half years and five grievance proceedings later, he quit.

*   *   *   *   *   *

Ron "Rambo" Battle had seniority and, by all rights, should have been in line for the available supervisory position. But his hard-nosed, abrasive style had already made him too many enemies to make his promotion possible. He had been passed over before, always with excuses that didn't quite ring true and that made him resentful. Ace Johnson was his new manager and did not relish having to confront him, but he felt it was time to face the problem directly. He tried to bring it up in his weekly one-on-one with Rambo, and was not prepared for the response. "That's a bunch of crap! I could supervise rings around any of 'em around here. It's the same old bull, and I won't forget it!" As Rambo stormed out of the office, Ace was wishing he had never brought it up. He now had an enemy working for him.

So what's a manager to do? Sure, you can be as hardnosed as you please and as your authority allows you to be, if you don't mind risking discontent, resentment, and a desire for revenge. Conversely, you can avoid the conflict by establishing "mafia pacts" with the difficult individuals: "You don't bother me too much; I don't bother you." But this only increases tension and frustration within your organization and within yourself. Either way, you're likely to wind up standing around that baggage carousel with that sinking feeling—no more bags are coming down the chute, all the other passengers on your flight have dispersed to the taxicab lines and rental-car lots, and you've got a meeting on Michigan Avenue in an hour. Meanwhile, some indifferent customs official in Tokyo is tossing your suitcase and your garment bag into the unclaimed property locker.

Employees may not send your bags to Japan. Often the best way to get even with a boss is to do just enough work not to get fired, but not a bit more. If enough employees follow suit, they'll send you to Japan instead.

This is a book about making conflict and change work for you instead of against you; about making them an asset instead of liabilities.

This is a book about using conflict and change to make you a better leader.

This is a book about managing conflict and change through balance—the balance between caring and accountability, between support and constructive criticism, between tight and loose, between organizational loyalty and truth, between substance and style, between leading and listening. It is balanced management that allows us to use tension without allowing it to turn into warfare.

This is a book that can help you to develop managerial tools for dealing with tension assertively and decisively; that can guide you in influencing your colleagues without alienating them; that can show you how to lead your subordinates without breeding resentment and rebellion—a book that can help you avoid having you or your bags sent to Japan.

This is a book that does not claim to have all the answers. It does provide a mirror that entertains, stimulates, convicts, and instructs. It's practical without being dry. It's a starting point, not a complete treatise.

Throughout this book we'll be highlighting various key ideas as "keepers" at the end of each chapter. You might want to copy any such keepers you find to be appropriate to your interests and goals. Keep them in a notebook for occasional review.

KEEPERS

☐ Find a middle ground between doormat and steamroller.

☐ Being abusive gets your bags sent to Japan.

☐ Manage change and conflict or it will manage you.

CHAPTER ONE

Beating the Myth
of the Perfect Manager

"No one—not even you—gives one hundred-percent perfect performance every time. The business world belongs to the quick and the bold . . . not the perfect. It's the struggle toward perfection that counts."

—Richard S. Sloma

In dealing with change, as in other aspects of leadership, we are too often stymied by our ideal of perfection. The myth of the perfect manager dies slowly. Laying to rest your own version of it is the first step toward making conflict work for you.

And it is a myth, make no mistake about it. The only places where perfect managers exist are in educational movies and management-training books.

This book will not make you a perfect manager—you may just have to settle for being better.

The myth of the perfect manager persists largely because many well-meaning authors and trainers provide us with picture-perfect scenarios that promote unrealistic expectations. Any writer with an approach to sell and a good grasp of his or her subject can expound eloquently about its benefits. With carefully selected examples, the writer builds a case for the "universal" applicability of his or her particular answer. Then the manuscript is turned over to an editor who smooths out the rough edges and corrects the obvious errors.

In training videos, people are working from a script, and they can shoot the scene over and over again until they get it right. The trainer's need to impress leaves the reader or the viewer with a sense of awe and renewed hope, along with a new set of expectations of what a good manager has to do to be effective.

These expectations are so tied up with perfection that no one can possibly live up to them. As a consequence, any training designed to help today's manager runs the risk of becoming more of a liability than an asset. It creates yet another list of "shoulds": a pattern of behavior that becomes cast in concrete as something that we must "always" follow if we wish to be effective.

> *"The only completely consistent people are dead."*
>
> —Aldous Huxley

Of course, in the real world the confrontation never seems to work out like the one in the book. Unlike the bright young manager in the training video, we don't have the luxury of a second or third take. It's usually about a half hour after the fact before most of us realize what we "should-a-said." Tired after a morning of crisis interruptions from important accounts, the real-world manager snaps at her secretary over a harmless question. Disconcerted by an edict from the board of education, the real-world school principal rips into one of his most valued teachers over a trivial point of protocol. Convinced that an effective administrator would "always know what to say," would "always have an open door" to subordinates, would "never lose control" with staff, they are left with one conclusion: "I must not be an effective manager! I need to go to another seminar! I need to read another book!"

Berry's World   **By Jim Berry**

"A mistake in judgment isn't fatal, but too much anxiety about judgment is."

—Pauline Kael

So what happens after the workshop is over? We come back all fired up with the ideal of perfection. Everyone expects us to act bizarre for a few days, and we do. But very soon we find ourselves drifting back in a downward spiral to our same old habits. Because we are so concerned with "doing it right," we avoid taking action for so long that we end up doing nothing at all. We become victims of the "Three Ps": Perfection, Procrastination, Paralysis. The executive declares to himself, "I hate my job," struggles to update his resume, becomes frustrated by his perceived shortcomings, and never sends it anywhere. The salesperson prepares new presentations, polishes them, reshapes them, begins to doubt herself, and never seems to find time to make the sales calls. The development director establishes a two-year task force to study a decision that ought to have been made in two weeks. The middle manager, eager for promotion, comes up with a brilliant idea, waits for the perfect moment to express it, and sees others get the credit for the idea—and the promotion that should have been his.

In the end, the seminar, the book, and the video, inspirational as they may have been, too often serve only to give us one more reason for whipping ourselves. In our society, friends, most of us are already very good at self-whipping and not nearly good enough at self-support. In a nutshell, demanding perfection from yourself can be dangerous to your health. Eric Berne, the well-known psychiatrist and author, put the problem in perspective. When asked to explain the difference between healthy and unhealthy people, he explained, "A healthy person goes 'Yes,' 'No,' and 'Whoopee!' An unhealthy person goes 'Yes, but,' 'No, but,' and 'No whoopee.'"

"Senior managers try to be explicit about our vulnerability and failings. We talk to people about the bad decisions we've made. It demystifies senior management and removes the stigma traditionally associated with taking risks. We also talk about the limitations of our knowledge, mostly by inviting other people's perspectives."

—**Robert D. Haas, CEO of Levi Strauss & Co.**

So what's the alternative? How do we drive the stake through the heart of this perfection vampire? How do we, as managers, avoid the pitfalls of the Three Ps?

Interestingly, even as the training people make us feel inadequate for being imperfect, the corporate cultures of so many of our most successful companies are moving away from the notion of perfection. Perfection is increasingly being viewed as out of place in today's environment of rapid and dramatic change, where today's perfection can be tomorrow's obsolescence. Instead, organizations are taking errors into account as part of the process of growth and development. One IBM executive suggested, "If I don't let people make mistakes, there is no ownership whatsoever." The CEO of a smaller, but highly successful, computer-peripherals company puts it this way: "We tell our people to make at least ten mistakes a day. If you are not making ten mistakes a day, you're not trying hard enough." The "blooper" shows, popular on TV during the '80s, are indicative of this new attitude as well. You would never have found film studios putting their outtakes on the air as entertainment back in the '70s, when the media and the self-help books were sharpening everyone's image of perfection.

> *"In excellent companies there is no bureaucratic mumbo-jumbo. People are measured and paid regularly on the basis of merit. The only place where risks will be taken is where there is a safety net of human support when failures occur and rewards for success."*
>
> —Tom Peters

In fact, if you look beyond the training materials and seminars, you'll notice that the watchwords for today's manager are not perfection but the pursuit of excellence and incremental improvement. Instead of following a pattern of plan-plan-plan-plan-plan-fail, Tom Peters tells us successful companies today are following a course of try it, test it, fix it, try it again, adjust it. They're building a style that makes room for learning from one's errors instead of seeing them as a statement of one's inadequacy.

> *"The illiterate of the future are not those who can't read and write but those that cannot learn, unlearn, and re-learn."*
>
> —Alvin Toffler, *Future Shock*

Let's face it, most of us find it a lot easier to read a book than to put it

"Harvey, sometimes I think you're too cautious about life."

into action. And if the book gives us some notion of the way a mythical, "perfect" manager is supposed to handle change, it's easy enough to say, "Right, that's it. Tomorrow I'm going to talk to Charlie. I'm going to do exactly what the book says." Then tomorrow comes, and once again it's, "I've got to find another book!"

Instead of trying to set the stage for perfection, take a realistic look at what you can do to increase your effectiveness batting average. Instead of sinking back into the mire of Perfection, Procrastination, and Paralysis, develop a sense of being free to take a few risks—to be wrong and to learn from it.

> *"The man who makes no mistakes does not usually make anything."*
>
> —Bishop W.C. Magee

After all, the effective managers are those who have made a commitment to improve their ability to influence and to motivate others. In being expressive and supportive, they make room for their own humanness, continuing to learn and to grow along with the people they work with. They do not always do things perfectly, but they do things. They do not always say profound things, but they say something. They can laugh and be serious; they can be inconsistent and still know how to follow through on important priorities. They can be firm and, at times, flexible. They don't have to be anything; they are able to be effective and realistic.

Never let the freedom and challenge to grow become an obligation to be perfect. There is no such thing as a perfect manager.

QUESTIONS WORTH ASKING

"At our company, producing quality products is one of our main goals. One of the things we keep stressing is, 'Do it right the first time.' Does that promote the myth of perfection or is it an appropriate emphasis?"

Risktaking and errors will always be a part of good product development, but it is the company's job to keep those errors from impacting customers. Emphasizing "Do it right the first time" is an appropriate emphasis for production quality control. It would not be a theme song for research and development. Even in production, one hundred-percent perfection is seldom a reality; a realistic goal is to minimize legitimate human and mechanical error, and to stand behind your products in servicing any problems that result.

KEEPERS

☐ Avoid the Three Ps: Perfection, Procrastination, Paralysis.

☐ Trade "Plan-plan-plan-fail" for "Try it, test it, fix it, try it again, adjust it until it works."

CHAPTER TWO

Beating the Myth of Winners and Losers

"Success and failure. We think of them as opposites, but they're really not. They're companions—the hero and the sidekick."

—Laurence Shames

This chapter examines the problem of how we handle those times when nothing seems to go right. If you never have days when you feel like a failure, never feel adversely affected by rejection, and never personalize such experiences so that they affect your ability to take risks, skip this chapter and jump ahead to the next one.

Did we lose anyone? I don't think so. We all have days when we feel like losers, and too often we let that feeling affect the way we do our jobs. But our typical notion of winners and losers is only a myth. The chief difference between winners and losers, as Sydney J. Harris tells us, is that winners lose more often than losers. They lose more often, but they also win more often because they don't let a loss put them out of the game.

Too many of us drop out of the game because of the idea that a "winner" is someone who *never* loses. It's part of our great American obsession with winning. A single loss can make one "a loser." We apply it to sports as well as to personal achievement. The team that fails to win the Super Bowl or World Series is a team that "could have made it, but failed."

For such a team to consider itself a failure is ludicrous. And yet we apply this same unrealistic standard to ourselves. It's not only ludicrous, it's downright self-destructive. It causes us to drop out of the game in frustration and despair. If you drop out of the game you can't lose, but you're guaranteed to be a loser.

Wayne Gretsky, the record-shattering hockey player, credits an early coach for helping to instill in him a winning attitude. The coach, frustrated by Wayne's sudden reluctance to shoot the puck, reminded him,

"You miss one hundred percent of the shots you never take." In the Oscar-winning classic, *Chariots of Fire,* the actor playing British Olympic champion Harold Abrahams declares after losing a race, "I run to win, and if I can't win, I won't run." The response of his lover brings him back to the reality that we all face: "If you don't run, you can't win."

> *"Failure does not count. If you accept this, you'll be successful. What causes most people to fail is that after one failure, they stop trying."*
> —Howard Newburger and Marjorie Lee

Let's face it, in any area of life, there is no substitute for results. Salesmen want to make sales. Leaders want good performance from their team. Parents want their children to act responsibly. Companies want their bottom-line figures in black ink. In all cases people have a clear idea of the results that for them would constitute winning—including you. You want to be liked. You want people to do their jobs. Often you want to be able to change people's minds, to sway their thoughts and influence their actions. You want your boss to buy your ideas, and your clients to be satisfied and to continue to buy. Getting results (winning) is an appropriate goal. There is pleasure in achieving victory. It's certainly a lot more fun than losing. It is this competitive urge to finish as a winner that pushes and challenges us to new heights. In the world of business, a history of winning the battle of the bottom line will make or break you and your company. Few would argue with the goal of producing a winner.

You want to win, and as a manager you feel that your position of authority puts you in control. But it is important to recognize that you can never hold all the cards. You cannot control others; at best, you influence them. We do not even motivate others; we establish a context that invites their own motivation. Our only "control" is over what we do to make winning probable. We can control only our own efforts and even that is in question on Monday mornings. Maximizing our influence batting average means embracing the new "Three Ps": Position, Perform, and Persist.

> *"I am not judged by the number of times I fail but by the number of times I succeed, and the number of times I succeed is in direct proportion to the number of times I can fail and keep on trying."*
> —Tom Hopkins

The winners of the world know the value of **positioning** for opportunity. By keeping up with trends in our field and anticipating changes, we can be in a position to take advantage of changes. That is not just waiting for "good luck;" it is planned positioning that helps make "luck" happen. Major league baseball teams will keep statistics on the hitting of their opponents and position their fielders where batters most often hit. That's smart positioning. My great uncle, Harvey Swanson, had another way of making the same point, "It's easiest to ride a horse in the direction it's going." He added an important corollary, "If the horse is dead, get off it!"

It's the same in business. You can be good at something no one wants. You can try to sell something no one now has a need to buy. That's poor positioning!

> *"By failing to prepare, you are preparing to fail."*
>
> —Benjamin Franklin

Unfortunately, even with the best of planning we miss the mark. Even with pinpoint pitching and positioned fielders, good hitters still find a way to get hits. Sometimes our luck turns sour. One can study future trends and demographic data for months and still miss key elements no one could account for. All crystal balls are by their nature foggy and open to error. None of us are always in the right place at the right time. Sometimes we guess wrong. Sometimes even your best efforts will fall short of the goal. The upsetting fact remains we don't control winning results, but we must work to influence them to make them the best possible. The winners of the world also know the value of constantly improving **performance.**

Positioning is critical in today's changing world, but positioning is not sufficient to sustain a winning bottom line. Just as companies need to constantly upgrade the quality of their products and services to compete, leaders must make a commitment to lifelong learning for themselves and their people. Good leaders continually invest time, energy, and training dollars in the incremental improvement of needed skills. They never stop searching for ways to improve. Leaders can't ask employees to prepare to meet the challenge of change without modeling that themselves.

> *"When you rest, you rust."*
>
> —Martin Luther

Richard L. Mooney has provided us with the following model that helps illustrate the interaction of **performance** and **positioning** on results. It shows the balance that typically exists among the possible outcomes. Quadrant 1 represents bad luck with bad performance—a sure recipe for **DISASTER**. In short, you didn't do your job and luck didn't save you. It's your job as a manager to keep this quadrant as small and as far away from your customer as possible. If this quadrant gets too large, take it personally. You are either not positioning yourself or you're not consistently doing your job. If your disasters are too frequent, perhaps management is not for you. But everyone, even under the best of circumstances, will have their disaster days. When we feel we're on a negative roll, we keep hoping it's only *Candid Camera* playing an ugly trick. It seldom is. As one manager so aptly expressed, "Some days you're the bug, and some days you're the windshield." Everyone has those days. Just work to keep them to a minimum and keep them from impacting customers.

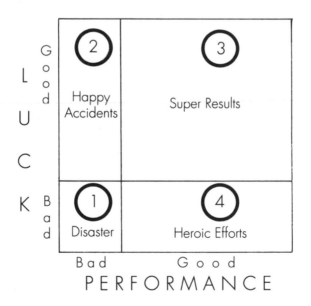

Then there are those times luck is your only salvation. If you perform poorly but have good luck, you land in Quadrant 2. You had a **HAPPY ACCIDENT.** You didn't do your job, but you still came out smelling like a rose. These also tend to be the times when your boss tells you, "Good job!" and you say to yourself, "If you only knew what I did!" Call it "career karma." It makes up for those other times when you should have won, but didn't. Take the victory, but don't take credit for it. Sometimes we win and we ought to be self-critical: "I was lucky. Next time I'd better handle it differently."

Quadrant 3 represents the optimum situation: good performance and good luck combine to produce **SUPER RESULTS**. When a football team has skilled players at the key positions and the breaks are going their way, the sportscasters say, "The momentum is on their side." Unfortunately, most teams tend to have difficulty sustaining that momentum. Super results can set the stage for complacency. Teams can be so wrapped up in celebrating they fail to prepare and perform in a way to sustain a winning record. Only the great teams can sustain a dynasty from season to season. It's the same in business. A track record of super results can lead to problems for today's managers. It encourages the illusion of control and promotes complacency. It can lead managers (and their companies) to assume that such bottom-line results will continue indefinitely without continued effort and planned change. It encourages us to rest on our laurels; to stand pat; to fail to position ourselves for the next opportunity. In our rapidly changing world, the best forerunner to bankruptcy may very well be a good year. Never let you or your people rest on past successes; use the good times to position and prepare for your continued victories.

When we perform well but luck just isn't on our side, our results fall into Quadrant 4. You did your job, but factors outside your control meant that you didn't get the results you deserved. Everyone has days when their good performance is not enough to overcome bad luck. Surgeons struggling unsuccessfully to save a patient perhaps understand this best of all. Doctors have a term to describe a good performance that ends in bad results: they call it **HEROIC EFFORTS**. They certainly feel a deep disappointment and a sense of loss, but they can't allow themselves to personalize the loss. If they did, the real loser would be their next patient.

"I claim not to have controlled events, but confess plainly that events have controlled me."

—Abraham Lincoln

Reprinted by permission of United Feature Syndicate, Inc.

In the business world heroic efforts seldom get the support they deserve. Too many managers quickly personalize all bad results, even bad results they did not cause. In our private moments, we assume intrinsically that we are somehow at fault: "Something is wrong with me—*I'm a loser!*"

This internal programming is a result of conditioning that most of us have been subjected to since childhood, like a rat being given a jolt of electricity each time it fails to run the maze properly. As kids, we had frustrated parents hollering at us for things we couldn't control. In playground games, losing was a sin; for missing a free throw or muffing a grounder, an eight-year-old child can be made to feel like Mrs. O'Leary's cow.

Then came dating (our first sales experience) a trauma to boys and girls alike. Remember? You wanted desperately to be asked out, or for your "askee" to accept. When you were turned down, you were quick to assume the burden of rejection: "It's my fault! There's something wrong with me! I thought I was covering it up, but she can see what I'm really like!" Few of us as teenagers were secure enough to give ourselves an equally plausible explanation: "The fool! She doesn't know something good when she sees it!" Many of us were so concerned about rejection and felt like dropping out of the game entirely for the rest of our high school years.

Now we're adults, but our programming remains. We still tend to take refusal as rejection and see ourselves as losers for it. Few of us find it easy to change that early, inner programming toward personalizing our losing efforts. If I try everything I know as a manager, and it doesn't work, I'm a lousy manager. If I try everything I know as a parent, and my kid doesn't come out as programmed, I'm a lousy parent! In reality, it's usually not true. However, there are people who can't work well with any manager. There are children who resist parenting, even from good parents. How many families do you know with two kids, one of whom gives their parents no trouble while the other drives them up the wall? And yet our society tells us that it's the parent's fault; it's the teacher's fault; it's the department manager's fault. It's always someone's fault, as if we had control over anyone but ourselves.

And so we continue to interpret disagreement as a personal attack, a subordinate's poor performance as a sign of our inadequacy as a manager, a child's irresponsible behavior as an indication of our failure as parents. And, unfortunately, when bad results lead us to label ourselves as losers, we tend to stop doing the very things that make it possible for us to become winners. We stop asking for what we want. We become hesitant in sharing new ideas. We find excuses not to make the sales call. We avoid our "problem people." We drop out of the game.

"If you want to have a good idea, have a lot of them."

—Thomas Edison

What we must realize is that the "game," by its very nature, involves a high level of frustration. *People are going to say no.* It's a fact of the world we live in, and it's more prevalent today than ever before. In business, any number of factors may prevent us from getting what we want; cost containment, budgeting pressure, pending reorganization, the challenge of excellence, the idea that we can't have more people and have to get by with the ones we've got. These facts are so plainly true they're practically in the death-and-taxes category, yet we personalize them as reflections on our competence, on our ability to control. It's even more true in education and health care, where funding is often at crisis level. We aren't getting new people; we have to get by with "motivating" the people we're left with. Yet when we're met with resistance, we drop out of the game by avoiding the difficult people. As a result, they generally can get away with what they want. And there we are, once more feeling as if we're going about with a big, red "L" for loser pinned to our lapel.

"Do what you can, with what you have, where you are."

—Theodore Roosevelt

This brings us to the final P: **Persist**. The winner is the man or woman who does not personalize poor results; they stay in the game! Such a person can be disappointed without feeling like a failure. Dr. Charles Garfield of the University of California Medical School in San Francisco conducted a study of fifteen hundred high achievers in business, science, sports, the professions, and the arts. He found that not one of the peak performers he studied defined losing as failing. They called their losses "setbacks," or "course corrections." Winners see refusal not as a personal rejection but as a problem-solving challenge. To effective salespeople, "no" is "on" spelled backwards. They may lose a few sales, but they win many, because they keep making the calls that make it possible. And we're all salespeople, whether we're selling a product, an idea, or ourselves.

"God grant me the serenity to accept the things I cannot change, the courage to change the things I can, and the wisdom to know the difference."

—Reinhold Niebuhr

The myth of winners and losers is the belief that a winner must bat a thousand. The real winner is the one who stays in the game, learns to play it well, accumulates a high batting average, and knows that a perfect one is only a fantasy. When you find the game you're good at, don't allow your inner programming to convince you that you're a loser simply because you've fallen behind in the first inning, the first lap, the first confrontation in the workplace. Stay in the game. Welcome the challenge of becoming the winner you're capable of being.

QUESTIONS WORTH ASKING

"I can appreciate the value of 'heroic efforts,' but how do I get my boss to support them?"

Your best bet is to let your track record of good results carry you through the tough days with or without your boss's short-term support. Understandably, you can't expect bosses to be beaming with enthusiasm for losing; no matter what your effort, you lost. It is also easy to understand why most frustration goes downhill; in the real world, it's seldom received well upwards. When was the last time your boss suggested a dumb idea, and you said, "Did you think before you said that?" It may be tempting, but you seldom express it.

Be realistic. What I hope for is a boss that will be frustrated "along with me" instead of "at me." Take the time to discuss what you did, not just your results.

Be open to suggestions and support. Learn to accept an occasional bad day from your boss; our mistakes do not always hit them at the best time. Usually, most come to appreciate our heroic efforts. When thinking of how poorly you have been handled at times, don't forget to pass some of that understanding on to those who work with you.

"Isn't there a point at which blaming things on bad luck becomes an all too handy excuse for not doing your job?"

Of course. Like an effective surgical team, most of us have been involved in legitimate heroic efforts. But at the same time, if a surgical team seldom saved a patient, we would not call their efforts heroic; we would hope that they would take up some other profession. As W.C. Fields so aptly said, "When at first you don't succeed, try, try again. Then quit! Don't be a damn fool about it!"

There *is* a time to get out of the game: When an honest evaluation of your performance brings you to a decision that you're in the wrong game. Not everyone is meant to be a surgeon, star hockey player, or an Olympic runner. Not everyone is meant to be a manager. If you never seem to get the results you want, and your skills just don't seem to be developing, even with training, find another game. Don't give up prematurely on the basis of having kept yourself out of the game for so long; but don't bang your head against a wall, either. Find games for which you have the skills and motivation to play.

As one manager said of her secretary, "To err is human, but she's just *too* human!" If you're finding yourself "too human," explore frankly the possibility that you may be in the wrong job. Don't spend years trying to tunnel your way through a mountain when there's an easy pass into the valley beyond. Learn to match your position to your skills. That secretary who was just "too human" became one of her company's best sales representatives.

KEEPERS

- ☐ You miss one hundred percent of the shots you never take.

- ☐ Winners win and lose more frequently than losers because they stay in the game.

- ☐ "No" is "on" spelled backwards.

- ☐ Position, perform, and persist to maximize results.

- ☐ Limit your "down time"; bounce back quickly from setbacks.

CHAPTER THREE

Excellence Is an Inside Job: Manage Yourself So You Can Lead Others

"If I am not for myself, who will be for me? If I am only for myself, what am I? And if not now, when?"

—Rabbi Hillel

Nowhere is self-confidence more important than in leading others, especially in confrontational situations. If we doubt ourselves, conflict becomes a never-ending cycle of avoidance, retreat, and self-doubt. We establish "comfort zones" from which we emerge to confront problems only if we are dragged out kicking and screaming. There is little chance that we can establish an environment in which others can motivate themselves if we aren't effective in motivating our own selves.

Unfortunately, most of us are ineffective in maintaining our self-confidence. On a daily basis we take the time to evaluate our own performance, what we like and don't like about what we've done. Our self-confidence at any given moment tends to be an inference from our most recent collection of private ratings. And for most people, the vast majority of our self-evaluations are negative.

If you're thinking that this doesn't apply to you, take a look at your own experience. It is very important to understand how this inner game works and to understand why so many of us privately major in self-deprecation. Can you think of five situations during the past week in which you were conscious of your own effectiveness? Driving home from work, do you ever glow inwardly about something you did or said that was indicative of what a terrific problem solver you are? Ever lose a night's sleep thinking about how well you handled that confrontation with Charlie? When was the last time you patted yourself on the back for a job well done?

If you're like most people, the answers to those four questions are: "No," "No," "No," and "I don't remember." We simply don't pay much attention to what is working. Instead, we tell ourselves, "I was lucky." "It's what I'm paid for." "It's about time; I should have done this weeks ago." "It could have been better." The good things that we do stay with us maybe eight seconds; it's our nagging mistakes that stick around for weeks. One error on the job is worth a good forty-five minutes of self-whipping spread out over a three-day period. Do any of these self-evaluations sound familiar? "That was dumb!" "I can't believe I said that!" "That's going to cost me!" "I stuck my foot in my mouth all the way up to the hipbone!" "[Expletive deleted], am I stupid! *And they were all watching me!* They're all going to go home tonight and write books about me!"

Reprinted by permission of United Feature Syndicate, Inc.

To make matters worse, it's a rare occurrence simply to experience the disappointment of a mistake. Most of us add a touch of torture by mulling it over for hours. We all have lost sleep over mistakes that triggered what seemed like an endless review of similar past failures and future disaster scenarios. One manager, in discussing this problem with me, likened it to a filer in the back of his brain. Every time he put himself down, his filer produced sheaves of evidence for the prosecution. The filer wasn't too precise, but he knew how to find the evidence: "Wait a second, boss. Let me look at your 'Dumb' file. Oh, yes, you *are* dumb.

Reprinted by permission of United Feature Syndicate, Inc.

Here's the record of that other time when you . . . We'll just file this one away to keep the evidence current. Hey, boss, at least you were right about one thing—you are stupid!"

Dr. David Rubin suggests that what we recall under such circumstances is affected not only by our real past experiences but also by our personalities and our beliefs about ourselves. As time passes we remember even false events better than the truth if they fit our image of ourselves. And if that image is predominantly negative, the results are predictable: self-doubt, depression, wasted time, decreased effectiveness, continued low self-confidence, and feelings of helplessness.

With such friends as ourselves, who needs enemies? In fact, if we gave ourselves a fraction of the support that we give to others in their times of crisis, we'd be far better off. A subordinate could file a grievance, and win, if abused the way we inwardly abuse ourselves. If a friend comes to you for consolation over a mistake or a foot-in-mouth episode, do you ridicule him? Do you pull the boy-were-you-dumb number? Do you list his similar past failures? Of course not. You say things like, "It's okay; don't worry about it." "We all make mistakes. That's why they put erasers on pencils." "It's no biggie! I've done the same thing myself." Many of us were brought up on, and may still believe in, the religious principle that one should "love thy neighbor as thyself." But the fact is we'd be far better off if we loved ourselves as we loved our neighbors!

To compound the problem, few of us are comfortable about admitting our internal self-assessment to others. With our burden of self-doubt, we can't afford to. We are too afraid of losing the respect of our friends, loved ones, and colleagues. The reason you don't see other people being overly self-critical is the same reason they don't see it in you. Publicly, we all try to put our best foot forward. We present ourselves as being ninety-five percent effective. If we admit to an occasional mistake, it's just to prove we're human. We get up in the morning, groom ourselves like fashion models, "dress for success"; and we screen most of our inappropriate or "dumb" public comments. The only person you know privately is yourself. As a result, when you compare your private self-image to everybody else's public image, you lose. You lose badly. It's not surprising that everyone else looks normal.

Psychologists who have studied this pervasive self-image problem in both men and women have called it "the impostor phenomenon." Dr. Joan Harvey of the Pennsylvania School of Medicine sums it up succinctly: "People who have trouble enjoying success often feel like frauds." In many cases, the more people achieve, the more they feel like phonies; that their success is undeserved; that the good things they do are invalid; that they somehow don't count. Have you ever caught yourself saying, "If anyone knew how much I don't know, I'd be in deep trouble"? You and everyone else!

HERMAN®

"Mind your own business! This is how I like it."

"So remarkably perverse is the nature of man that he despises those that court him and admires whoever will not bend before him."

—Thucydides

Even the most successful people do not always feel successful. It is easy for managers to undervalue their own strengths. In their attempts to prove themselves, they climb onto a never-ending treadmill, and in the process it's easy to lose a sense of their own self-worth. Many may project confidence and even brag about their effectiveness, but it's often just a cover for feelings of inadequacy, feelings they can't let anyone see. In the most severe cases, if you confront such a person about a problem you're having with them, fifteen minutes later you're trying to figure out how it somehow became your fault. They've learned through years of practice how to make everything someone else's fault. They are so afraid that someone will find out they're imposters that they must hide behind a facade of perfection. They tend not to develop confidence in subordinates; they are too threatened by effective people. They may go to a therapist but let no one know about it; they wear sunglasses and pay in cash. As vain as they may seem, these unfortunates may be candidates for nervous breakdowns, early heart attacks, or worse.

When your self-confidence is low and your assessment of others unrealistically high, you have a tendency to crave the approval of others: your boss, peers, subordinates, friends, spouse, and children. Let's face it, when you major in self-criticism, you need a lot of support just to break even! But that's a trap. If you must have the approval of others, they are ultimately in control of your self-confidence. If that approval is taken away, you tend to become distressed and less than effective.

> *"I care not what others think of what I do, but I care very much about what I think of what I do! That is character!"*
>
> —Theodore Roosevelt

In a world filled with conflict and change, a good manager can't afford to hand over that kind of control to any other person. She needs the ability to weather the storm of disapproval in pushing through an unpopular change; to be able to disagree with a boss and sometimes to confront difficult, negative employees. He needs to be able to admit his own mistakes and bounce back quickly to solve a problem instead of hiding from accountability. Too often results are sacrificed for the need to save face; time is lost blaming others instead of dealing with the real problems. Without a realistic, balanced self confidence, it is hard to take the risks necessary to be effective. It is too easy to allow the need to be well liked to take precedence over other, vital, managerial concerns.

When that happens, productivity and morale suffer. Dr. David McClelland of Harvard University has found that managers with such a strong need for approval will tend to be controlled by their most difficult employees. They will make exceptions for the difficult people, alienating other workers by undermining their faith in the merit-reward system. Ultimately, they lose credibility with both. If you are vulnerable to the approval of others to such an extent, you'll be seriously limited in your ability to do your job.

> *"No one can make me feel inferior but myself."*
>
> —Eleanor Roosevelt

You deserve better. You deserve to be managed by yourself in the same way you would manage others. Armed with awareness of the self-deprecation game (and with the fact that many of the hard-charger types you envy are playing it too), you can learn to make room for your mistakes and your strengths. The task of maintaining a realistic self-confidence will challenge you in two areas. First, you will need to increase the frequency and quality of your self-support; you will have to catch yourself being effective. Second, you will need to replace your negative ruminations and self-whipping with specific, constructive self-criticism that will help you benefit from every mistake.

Building a realistic self-confidence begins with an ability to cultivate appropriate self-support. This is not an open invitation to join the "me generation" or to cultivate a swelled head; it is a challenge to you to build an internal balance, to know your strengths, and to learn from your mistakes. You may be winning and have no awareness of it because you're only recording the losses. You can't know that you're winning unless you're keeping an accurate score of your goals and achievements.

Setting and achieving goals is one of the dynamics that make the world work. It is an effective motivator and should remain so for you and for the people responsible to you. Goal-setting allows us to strive for new heights; it keeps people and organizations vital. A person without new challenges can easily slide into a life of boredom. A company without goals can easily slip into bankruptcy. Effective managers will continue to set goals for themselves and their people.

> *"'I had a dream, I reached it. I lost the dream, and I miss it.' It was the same for our whole organization. We had a dream and we reached it, and we reached it very quickly. You see, it had all been a little too easy. And we created frustration, because this is a psychological game. Do you know the song Peggy Lee sings, 'Is That All There Is?' I learned that, before you reach an objective, you must be ready with a new one, and you must start to communicate it to the organization. But it is not the goal itself that is important."*
> —Jan Carlzon, CEO of SAS

We so much want to treat life as if it is a victory to be won instead of a journey to be lived well. As a leader, you need to be ready with the next goal for your people *and* yourself. Equally important to the process, however, is the need to balance goal-setting with appreciation of how far you've come. We need to be able to celebrate milestones along the way without resting there. The problem with goal-setting and achievement as the only source of self-confidence is that you never arrive. And unless you're aware of this little "catch-22," you find yourself hip-deep in self-deprecation without realizing how you got there. As a child, you were programmed for achievement through such tales as *The Little Engine that Could*. Remember: "I think I can, I think I can"? Only it doesn't work that way in real life. You may choo-choo up that mountain with all the self-confidence you can muster, but as you near the top, clouds begin to form, and a little turkey called "Boss" comes down out of the clouds and tells you, "Sorry, the hill is higher! Keep climbing!" And so you set yourself up for another round of self-whipping. If achievement is your only motivator, you're always behind, unappreciative of the balanced perspective of how far you've come.

Our victories are easily forgotten; the skills we use in achieving them we easily take for granted. They are like prized paintings that we hang on our walls. After two weeks of walking past them, we no longer even see them. We possess them but no longer experience them. We don't see the pictures again until we move, unless they are stolen or are brought to our attention by a guest seeing them for the first time. That's why we like to invite guests over; they show us our homes.

We do the same things with our skills. Things that were once difficult for us become easy and expected; we no longer count them as significant. Don't get complacent about your successes, but don't discount them, either. Continue to set new goals that allow you to grow, but take time regularly to browse through that attic and catch the things you do that make you effective. Self confidence comes out of a balance of striving for new achievements with ongoing recognition of your existing strengths.

Even on one of those days when nothing seems to go right, when your deadline for a project has just been moved up a week and you got a parking ticket besides, take the initiative to catch yourself being effective. You made a mistake on the Hinckley account, but you listened to his tantrum without losing your cool. Be good to yourself on those tough days and you won't stay down long. You'll be creating your own momentum, the momentum you need to bounce back.

> *"I found five thousand ways how not to make a light bulb."*
> —**Thomas Edison**

Don't confuse self-confidence with blind positivism. Not everything we do has positive results; it is an inescapable fact that we are going to make mistakes. In building realistic self-confidence we have to leave room for appropriate self-criticism. The trick is to give ourselves the luxury of talking to ourselves the way we would talk to someone we care about. Avoid the name-calling that invites a negative self-image and a recounting of past failures. Few people can fairly be categorized as good or bad, creative or dull, responsible or flaky, effective or ineffective, indispensable or deadwood. Each of us is a blend of many characteristics; we all have times when our behavior matches each of those descriptions.

Cultivate a theory of yourself in which you see your mistakes as the exception rather than the rule. Don't call yourself "dumb" just because you haven't handled a given situation well. Focus instead on specific behavior: "I didn't handle that confrontation well. Next time I'll handle it differently." "That's not like me. Most of the time I'm more responsible than that." Specific self-criticism will help you minimize self-whipping; generalized self-criticism invites long sessions of rummaging in your past-failure files. It's easier to admit you made a mistake than to assume you are one. It's easier, it's more honest, and it's far healthier.

> *"Mishaps are like knives, that either serve us or cut us, as we grasp them by the blade or the handle."*
>
> **—Herman Melville**

Of course positive self-criticism sounds easier in a book than it will be in actuality. You can learn to focus your self-criticism and minimize your down time by resorting to one of the two most effective forms of cheap therapy—a friend or a journal. Our ancestors knew how to use both of these mental-health aids to maintain their sanity long before there were therapists. The sting of self-whipping can be soothed by the process of talking out or writing down your feelings about it. Try a friend or colleague you know will support you but will still help you honestly to deal with your drawbacks. The more effective you become at managing yourself, the more open you will be to other people's criticism and the more able you will be to use it. If you prefer to keep your negative feelings private, try putting them down on paper rather than allowing them to echo for hours inside your head. After writing down your thoughts (and after you've given yourself a chance to let the dumb-dumb-dumb reverberations die down), read them over to yourself. You will find it easier to move on to a more constructive self-evaluation.

In considering your mistakes, use these questions and responses as a guide:

What did I do specifically that I do not approve of? (That's not like me. I don't like the way I. . .)

How would I like to handle it in the future? (Next time, I would. . .)

Is there anything I can do now to fix the problem?

If "yes," is it worth the cost in time or possible repercussions?

If "yes," establish a plan and set a date to initiate the follow-through.

If the answer to either of the last two questions is "no," let it go! But not without taking a moment to remember a time you handled a similar situation well. Relive that image of your positive history, and use the energy gained from the remembering to bounce back.

Some mistakes are costly. There is no need to condone them, but we can work through them to develop positive energy out of every error. A mistake can be seen either as a problem or an opportunity. When self-criticism is constructive it moves us forward toward problem-solving. You can never eliminate error, but you can work toward eliminating your preoccupation with it.

Life is a moving vehicle with no brakes and no reverse. With the pace of change, it's picking up speed. If you spend too much time looking in the rearview mirror, you'll hit a tree head on. This is why your front window is bigger than your rearview mirror. If you set realistic goals for achievement and balance self-support with appropriate self-criticism, you'll stay on the road. Managing your own self-confidence is a major step toward leading others. Keeping self-criticism fair, specific, and future-focused is half the battle. And it's not as hard as it may seem. After all, if you can manage to bring your self-perceptions up only as high as fifty-percent positive, you'll be miles ahead of the competition.

There is more to managing your own motivation than giving yourself balanced self-feedback and establishing high, but realistic goals. One of the keys to self-management may very well be your ability to generate a sense of purpose in what you do.

> *"Hardy Executives are self-confident and have a sense of purpose. They have the knack of making whatever they do feel important."*
>
> **—Salvatore Maddi, Ph.D.**

The power of purpose doesn't just help us succeed; it may also be one of the secrets to a long, healthy life. After following for seven years telephone executives adapting to the upheaval of corporate divestiture, Dr. Maddi and his colleague Suzanne Kobasa, Ph.D., found that the healthiest executives shared three characteristics: a feeling of *commitment*, a sense of *control* in their lives and an acceptance of life's stressful moments as *challenges*, rather than threats. Having a sense of commitment provides us with a sense of meaning, but it also seems to make us more resistant to the impact of today's stressful living.

We forget the importance of going internally to our own sense of purpose and to our memories of the people that helped teach us by the way they lived. Such internal journeys are not only free, they are guaranteed to fit the person. To add to the value of purpose-directed self-talk, such inspiration is instantaneously available every moment of every day if we would just take the time to think of them.

> *"Joy is not in things, it is in us."*
>
> —Ben Franklin

Joy and purpose are deeper than a feeling of happiness. Happiness depends on what happens to you; it's a function of the circumstances of the moment. Joy defies circumstance and is a choice of attitude to view every day through a filter of meaning and value. What are you committed to? What do you believe gives you a sense of purpose? Why do you work? What do you want to be remembered for by those who look to you for leadership? Who are the heroes and mentors you go to in your mind when you need inspiration?

Jack Nichols was the first manager Terry ever worked for; he was also the best. Terry was seventeen, a summer employee, helping to construct the Stanford Linear Accelerator, a big, mile-long, electron microscope. Terry was a lab technician; he drove a truck. Even though Terry was Jack's only summer employee, to Jack, he was still special. Jack had a prominent sign on his office wall that read, "Every person I work with knows something better than me. It's my job to listen long enough to find it and use it." Jack lived that message, scheduling a fifteen-minute walk with each of his team members every week. Terry's walk was on Friday. On his first walk, Jack asked Terry a *stupid* question, **"What's working for you?"** Shocked and unable to think of anything, Terry finally shared something he had learned from one of the other workers. Jack replied, "I'm glad you're learning from the guys, but I want you to know that I expect to learn something from you this summer. So I'm going to ask you this question every week." Jack did ask it every week, and Terry worked to make sure he had an answer for him every Friday.

I was that teenager, and Jack is one of my *heart leaders* that I go to when I need inspiration and direction from his model. Beyond the ideas Jack's style generated in me and other team members, I knew he believed in me. He helped me believe in myself. I think of him often and try to act the same way in leading others. Who are your *heart leaders* that helped you get where you are today and what can you learn from them?

> *"The most important thought that you can ever hold is: Your life matters."*
> —David McNally, *Even Eagles Need a Push*

There is no one blueprint of how the power of purpose works, it's a personal journey that each must make. Take the time to find your own road map. To the frantic days on the job, the hectic freeways, home demands, and interruptions interrupted by other interruptions, add a new priority. Take time to experience and celebrate your purpose and the people that have made you the person you are. Look for your own opportunities to make a difference on and off the job. Experience the power of your purpose.

> *"Everything can be taken from a man but one thing: the last of the human freedoms—to choose one's attitude in any given set of circumstances, to choose one's own way."*
> —Victor Frankl, Auschwitz prisoner and author of
> *Man's Search for Meaning*

QUESTIONS WORTH ASKING

"Can managing one's self-confidence be taken too far?"

Not if it's done responsibly. This chapter is not another call for the "me generation." When you're aware of your strengths and can accept your limitations, you're open to growth and are not threatened by the effectiveness of nor the feedback from others. True self-confidence is an inside job that reflects itself in an outer strength of character. There is little room for ego problems in a business world that requires consensus, participation management, and team effort. Responsible self-esteem leaves room for the strengths of all members of a team combining to produce a winning effort without any one member having to get all the credit. That is true self-confidence—strength with humility.

KEEPERS

☐ Catch yourself being effective.

☐ Treat yourself the way you treat others that you care about.

☐ Balance goal-setting with self-support.

☐ Be specific and future-focused in your self-criticism.

☐ Find the power of purpose and your *heart leaders*.

CHAPTER FOUR

Care Enough to Confront: Being Tough as Nails and Supportive

"We found that the most exciting environments—that treated people very well—are also tough as nails. There is no mumbo-jumbo. . . . Excellent companies provide two things simultaneously: tough environments and very supportive environments."

—Tom Peters

One of the reasons that conflict on the job can get out of hand is that we care too much. In our desire to avoid hurting someone's feelings, we allow a problem to escalate out of control.

To understand how this process works, imagine the following scenario. If the sport of basketball holds no interest for you, please be patient.

It's a crucial playoff game, the Lakers versus the Bulls. Magic Johnson and Michael Jordon have been going head to head since the opening tip. With two minutes to play and the score tied, the ball is passed to Magic. He moves to his left for a hook. Jordon holds his position and falls as Magic shoots. The ball bounces around the rim before settling in, but the action is stopped by the referee's whistle. "Number 42, charging! No basket!" he cries.

Magic turns on his heel. "Charging? What are you talking about?" he shouts. "He didn't have position! Are you blind? He was holding me!"

"Now, calm down, Magic," the ref says. "There's no need to make a big thing out of this. Let's sit down on the bench for a minute and talk this through like adults. I want to keep this a clean game. Michael, Magic says you were holding him. Did you . . ."

Jordon angrily cuts him off. "I hardly touched him! It was charging all the way! Don't let his Hollywood tears fool you!"

"Now, stop this, both of you," the ref pleads. "Now, one of you is lying. We are not resuming this game until we resolve this dispute." Turning to the fans, the ref pleads, "Now, you all saw what happened. How many of you think Magic was charging? How many think Michael was holding?"

Enough. This isn't basketball, it's a *Saturday Night Live* skit. In real life, sports officials know the rules and call the fouls as they see them. They don't expect their decisions to be popular. If they were easily intimidated by players, coaches, or fans, you'd have a very long game with a lot of commercials.

As a manager, you are often placed in the role of referee. Unfortunately, most managers don't want the job; they hate to call fouls. They have, however, one advantage over their black- and white-clad counterparts. Sports officials never get to say, "Good shot!" or "Here's an extra two points for being such a nice guy." If management were nothing more than calling fouls, we'd all end up with our bags sent to Japan. The question we all must consider, though, is what do we do when the fouls are committed? When two office "stars" square off? When a key player chronically complains and balks about team decisions? When a marginal player asks you to make exceptions? When corporate rightsizing requires difficult layoffs? How do we balance being "nice" with the necessity of maintaining a playing field that's fair to all concerned?

Most of us have been programmed since childhood to be caring and understanding. Remember, "If you can't say anything nice, don't say anything at all?" In our present age of psychological enlightenment, when many self-help books are often outselling novels, being nice often translates into accepting, if not condoning, the aberrant or counterproductive behavior of others. We pride ourselves on our sensitivity. The ability to understand, to care, and to empathize can be invaluable in helping us to make sense out of people's behavior. When a valued employee is undergoing a personal crisis, listening, patience, and directed counseling can often help him hold his own until he can turn things around and become a productive member of the team. Certainly only a heartless dictator would be completely insensitive to an employee whose problems have resulted in a temporary drop-off in effectiveness.

But it is equally true that leaders who are overly concerned with caring and understanding can easily fall into a trap in which they fail to hold team members accountable for their work performance. They move from understanding to tacit acceptance. The issue we must struggle with is how to avoid this trap, making room for understanding while at the same time maintaining accountability.

Joe Exacto is a graphic artist for *Trendsetter* Magazine. Joe is a fine artist when his personal life is going smoothly, which works out to be about one month out of three. The rest of the time he always seems to be involved in some personal crisis that affects his productivity. Ted Boardman, the art director at *Trendsetter,* has been patient with Joe, but he has learned that whenever Joe comes into his office and shuts the door behind him, it's a signal that there's a problem he needs to talk out. "My God," he thinks, as Joe recounts his latest tale of woe, "the guy must watch the soaps every day to keep coming up with new material!"

TED: . . .Well if it's that bad, maybe you'd better talk to Employee Assistance.

JOE: I can't do that; they'd find out! I can't let that happen! Once it's in the computer, anyone can find out!

TED: Those records are private. But if you're sensitive about that, what about finding your own therapist?

JOE: I can't afford one—not on the salary you pay me!

TED: Well, what about a clinic?

JOE: I don't believe in clinics.

TED: Well, what about a minister, or a priest, or a rabbi?

JOE: Don't believe in them either.

TED: Well, you can't keep going on like this; it's eating you up. You need someone to talk to.

JOE: I know. That's why I'm so glad I have you!

Have you ever felt like you've adopted an employee? Maybe this scenario is easier to relate to than the basketball game. Ted has fallen head-first into the caring and understanding trap. Our caring and understanding can provide the very excuses we need to avoid dealing with the problem, until one day we wake up and find that we've adopted someone like Joe. For teams to develop a natural synergy, everyone must carry their own load. Carrying Joe on an otherwise productive team stifles morale. The lesson is hard to learn; sometimes leaders have to confront people. For most of us, this is just not being "nice." It may not be "nice," but it is necessary. As Peters would suggest, managers have to balance being supportive with being tough as nails.

If you don't, the situation will only compound itself. You will find yourself making the most ludicrous rationalizations for avoiding the necessary conflict. Consider the situations faced by these "understanding" managers:

> Paula Mendoza was the chief administrative assistant to Bill Solomon, president of Solomon, David, and Bathsheba Advertising. In order to provide a summer job for his oldest daughter, Mona, Bill hired her to assist Paula. Mona's performance on the job could best be described as "steady": She spent most of her time motionless. What she did best was taking bathroom breaks and playing her radio. Paula attempted to find tasks for her, but she found that Mona's lack of follow-through created more problems than she was worth. It was pointless to talk to her; she was so spoiled that Paula was certain it would do no good. Besides, she just could not bring herself to come down hard on the boss's daughter. Her only hope was that Mona would change. Her only chance—fat.

*   *   *   *   *   *

> Sonny "Super Sell" Sunday was a top salesman for Cantaloni Corrugated. He had been with the company for twenty-four years and was a steady performer, but was noted for lack of concern about company policy. The sales support staff complained about his inadequate product specification reports and his arrogant demands for special privileges. Complaints to sales manager Lonnie Burch brought a constant refrain: "Well, you know Sonny. He's been that way for years, and he's not going to change. Don't take him seriously. After all, we can't afford to risk the loss of two million worth of accounts. Just humor him." After one battle too many with "good old Sonny," the product-design manager quit. So did some of the younger salespeople, who were outraged at the double standard that kept their accounts at a disadvantage. Because good old Sonny was "irreplaceable," Cantaloni Corrugated had to replace four promising young sales reps.

*   *   *   *   *   *

> The budget crunch was on in the Armadillo County School District. To save money, the superintendent decided that all vice principals would have to go back to the classroom on a part-time basis. Nearly all the district's VP's acceded to the ruling; some, to be sure, with greater reluctance than others. But Dorothy Dunder refused.

When the superintendent and her principal invited her in to talk, Dorothy started to cry. "It's okay," Superintendent Crosby said, trying to reassure her. "We've arranged so that you'll only have to teach one period a day." Now she was sobbing in great heaves. "Look," said Principal Hope, "We could make it an honors class with only seven students. But if you don't go back, we're going to have trouble with everybody else." By now Dorothy was beyond crying; she was hyperventilating. She slipped off her chair and onto the floor. The two men started to pick her up before they realized that they were touching a woman with no other women present. They dropped her. They opened the door and summoned a female secretary to assist as an observer. All three lifted Dorothy up and carried her past the secretarial pool to the nurse's office, where they quieted her down. Never again did they suggest to Dorothy that she go back to the classroom.

What is the lesson here? If assertiveness doesn't work, try hyperventilating? The lesson, of course, has nothing to do with crying Dorothy, or with steady Mona, or salesdog Sonny; it has to do with Paula, Lonnie, Hope, and Crosby. In each of these cases the managers were "understanding"; each had a way of rationalizing why the employee "could not" change and why he or she "could not" confront a serious work performance problem. But being an understanding manager is not the same as being an effective leader.

In Chapter 4 we cited Harvard's David McClelland on the problems that can arise when a manager is too preoccupied with being liked. The "nice" manager may end up being liked but not being respected. In Paula's case, her fear of confronting her boss or his daughter jeopardized her own standing within the company. Lonnie's decision to "let Sonny be Sonny" caused the loss of one manager and the erosion of his sales staff and its future. As for Hope and Crosby, what do you figure happened to the morale of the other vice principals in Armadillo County when they caught on that Dorothy was receiving special treatment?

"My management philosophy stresses team work, with each person being the boss in their particular area of responsibility. And they 'earn their space'—they earn the right to make mistakes, to make changes. Once in awhile the boss has got to escalate some priorities, but you have to leave room for people to put their fingerprint on things. If each person is allowed to do what he wants to do, he will do it well...in a way that will

help the team. As a Bell manager I probably fired more than anyone else—but always with a handshake because they were people who shouldn't have been in that job. I feel if you don't do a good job it's because you don't want to do it."

—Stan Daurio, President of Infolist Inc.

Your responsibility as a leader remains to challenge team members to be consistent, quality performance that maximizes results. When you consistently settle for less than acceptable performance from any of your employees, for whatever reason, you are not doing your job. Rather than caring enough to motivate your team, you are creating an environment that breeds "institutional anchors" that drag down the performance of your organization. By allowing such poor performance to continue without confronting the people responsible, you are participating in their failure.

"A stern discipline pervades all nature, which is a little cruel that it may be kind."

—Herbert Spenser

The following statements are typical of managers caught in the caring and understanding trap. Do you ever use excuses like these to avoid confronting your resident anchors?

"Your son-in-law's not here this afternoon. He's gone to your funeral."

"You know old Barney; he's been that way for years, and he's not going to change. You can't teach an old dog new tricks. If we're lucky, he'll retire soon, but until then we'll just have to pick up the slack."

"I get nowhere with Jim. We've been buddies for years, but ever since I was put in charge of the department, I feel he has used our friendship. He knows I haven't got the stomach to take him on."

"Every time I even suggest to Martha that she might have made a mistake, she goes off like a firecracker. She makes such a scene, I've learned to lay low unless it's really important. It just isn't worth it."

"I sometimes feel that Tricia is a walking *Perils of Pauline*. I just can't believe how one person can have such bad luck all the time. But I care about my staff, so I'll give her one more chance."

"Ralph has been a teacher here for a long time— too long, it often seems. He just isn't able to handle today's kids. Every time I walk past his classroom, it seems to be in an uproar. I don't know what good it would do to talk to him. He's been doing it his way for thirty-five years. As long as there are no complaints from parents, we might as well let him keep on doing it."

"I know that John has been coming in late from lunch with liquor on his breath. Sure, his judgement is slipping, and he's costing us, but you've got to understand that he's under a lot of pressure on the job and at home. Be patient with him. He promised me he'll get his drinking under control. He's been a good man for years; you can't let a few drinks spoil his record."

"Mary is the sweetest person you'll ever meet, but no matter how hard she tries, she just doesn't seem to have what it takes. I've sent her through training, but she's still not hacking it. I just don't have the heart to tell her."

"Sure, Tom is an inconsistent performer and he creates friction with some of the staff, but he's darn near irreplaceable in today's market. When he does perform, he's dynamite, and we can't guarantee that we could find anyone better."

Occasionally our reluctance to confront can lead us into uglier and more destructive rationalizations:

"He's black and he's lazy. You can't expect his kind to work. We've got to keep him on to humor the lawyers. If we tried to confront him, he'd file a grievance, and we'd be the ones on trial."

"Women are impossible! If you challenge them, they burst into tears or they call foul. If you try to act nice, they claim you're coming on to them. I don't want to be labelled a heartless SOB or a male chauvinist pig. I've learned to keep a low profile with the women around here; they're nothing but trouble."

Each of these statements employs labels that are convenient to use when we as managers can't confront and have convinced ourselves it wouldn't do any good anyway. If you read them with a critical eye, you will have noticed that few of these excuses have anything to do with caring. They're the result of managers falling into "learned helplessness"—nothing they do will make any difference, so why try. Others settle for "magical thinking," hoping that a problem will just go away by leaving it alone.

Many supervisors rely on inaction or magic instead of confrontation simply because they do not know or understand the correct legal ways of administering effective discipline. They have seen penalties backfire and heard about terminations that were overturned; they are afraid of involving their companies and themselves in a lawsuit. They so rarely administer discipline that they don't know how. Still other managers draw back from the tedious paperwork involved in their busy schedules as an excuse. In some cases they have not evaluated their employees accurately or honestly in the past; they have built a more positive record of their "anchors" than they deserve.

Of course, learned helplessness and magical thinking don't work. Most problem employees don't get challenged; they stay adopted. Whether the employee is old, young, oversensitive, irreplaceable, alcoholic, bellicose, or just plain weird; a man, a woman, a Boston Brahmin, or a member of a minority group; whether he/she has personal problems, family problems, or connections with the Chairman of the Board; as soon as we see them as people we can't confront, we are giving ourselves permission to do nothing. And be assured that if you do nothing, nothing will happen.

At least nothing positive will happen. The following are some of the reasons today's managers must care enough to confront their employees and hold them accountable:

Failure to hold all employees accountable places an unwarranted burden on your good team members.

If you have three productive workers and two anchors on your team, whom do you turn to when there is extra effort needed and deadlines to be met? *The anchors?* When your best workers quite reasonably tell you, "We've been working overtime every night this month. Why don't you give it to Rita?" we explain it away: "Well, you know Rita, she . . ." (Review the aforementioned excuses and choose your favorite.) You cast your bucket down a well for one reason—to get water. But when you drop it down the well of your problem people, you get no water; instead, they grab the bucket.

> *"I'm not a great motivator. I just get rid of the guys who can't motivate themselves."*
> —Lou Holtz, Notre Dame football coach

By avoiding the confrontation you sow the seeds of resentment, bitterness, and low morale in your good workers. The inequity of the situation can result in burnout or turnover. And when the good people leave, who are you left with? The anchors! They never leave. Why should they? They don't have to work. Of course, if you can't find anybody good to do the extra job, don't worry—you can always do it yourself!

By not demanding accountability, you fail to protect people from their own incompetence.

Effective employee discipline is not meant to punish, but to inform. If you really care about the people responsible to you, consider that their difficulties might mean they're in the wrong job. They may have been pocketed into a position within the organization which represents their level of incompetence. Care enough to confront them strongly long before their job is in jeopardy.

In the right work environment, they could come to life. By letting them stumble along out of some notion of "understanding," you're not doing them any favors. Ultimately, a person often knows when he's not doing his job. For people who care about their work, this can be a living death. Because you hesitate to hold them accountable, your problem remains unsolved, and their self-esteem drops through the floor.

By failing to act consistently, you can make it more difficult to fire people when the time comes.

Most managers who are reluctant to confront finally do get tough once the situation has deteriorated to the point where a worker has to be fired. But by then you may find that you have painted yourself into a legal corner. Lawsuits for wrongful dismissal are proliferating; courts in various states have imposed restrictions against "employment at will." They have begun to uphold implied contractual agreements between employees and workers where none have existed. Through your caring and understanding you have consistently given an employee positive evaluations, firing her may turn into an expensive hassle. The personnel manager will come to you with the employee's file and say, "Where's the documentation?"

"Documentation, hell! She's just not cutting it."

"But look at the evaluations you wrote for her last year; they were fine. You gave her a three-percent raise."

What do you say then—"I was lying"? You have made the personnel manager the employee's advocate. If you have not held your employees consistently accountable, you have not been doing your job. Consistency sends a strong, clear message. Does seeing a police car when you're driving affect your right foot? It does mine! I've found his giving a ticket is not a threat, it's a promise. As a result, we pay attention.

Inconsistent management almost invites testing of limits. It's similar to the difference between a slot machine and a vending machine. You can lose hundreds of dollars in a progressive slot machine. You're never sure whether your next three bucks will score the big win or whether it'll just be another three bucks down the tube. When you test an inconsistent manager you aren't sure whether you will be counseled or whether they will look the other way. Such managers are tested constantly. But if a slot player were to put money into a vending machine and no cola came out, what would she do? She'd jiggle the coin-return lever, kick the machine, and complain to the management. In any case, she wouldn't chuck any more coins into the machine and say, "Pretty soon this baby is going to pay off!" Anything that is consistent gives you immediate information, in this case, that the machine is broken. Consistent managers don't vacillate. They promise their people: I will hold you accountable *every time!*

Your employees deserve to know that you will react consistently to their departures from acceptable performance. Don't issue threats; make promises. If you have been through one confrontation with a problem individual and have made it clear what the consequences of a repeat performance would be, back up your words with appropriate action.

The goal of discipline should be to *retain a valuable employee, not to fire him.* Before an employee's job is in jeopardy, a manager has the opportunity to provide at least four or five stages of consistent follow-through to prove that she means what she says. That's the way it should be. You don't want to lose an employee; replacing him and training someone new is costly to all concerned. That gives you the opportunity to be supportive, to provide positive feedback, and to demonstrate caring and understanding. By just looking the other way, you only participate in his failure.

You will never be able to be consistent in all areas, nor would you want to be that controlling. Be loose in the areas where you want employee initiative and innovation. Provide tight controls in the critical performance areas where mistakes are costly.

When you fly coast-to-coast, you trust that the airline has maintained quality control with its pilots and equipment, especially with regard to maintaining altitude. If the pilot didn't stay above eight thousand feet while crossing New Mexico, you'd participate in the Rocky Mountain High experience in a way you'd just as soon avoid! Below that altitude, does it matter how hard the pilot is trying? You have participated in his failure. And so have his managers if they have looked the other way and failed to confront the problem.

By being reluctant to confront their marginal employees, many managers inadvertently allow performance that can result in critical errors. Know your eight thousand-foot level for your employees. Know the point at which people are not performing. It is your responsibility to hold them accountable.

"Things have changed. When you had forty-eight men you could carry a drunk or two, but no more."

—An anonymous tanker chief mate
who sails near Valdez, Alaska

You can be held personally liable for employees' mistakes.

In Lansing, Michigan, two nursing-home administrators were indicted for criminal negligence in the death of a patient. The facility had been cited before for improper care, and the court determined that the administrators had done nothing to hold their employees accountable.

In Austin, Texas, three construction-company officials, including the CEO, were indicted on charges of criminally negligent homicide as the result of a cave-in that killed two construction workers.

In Maywood, Illinois, three chemical-company officers were convicted of murder and each was sentenced to twenty-five years in prison for the death of a factory worker by cyanide poisoning.

In a case that has been called the "Aberdeen Decision," three civilian

CROCK

By permission of Bill Rechin, Don Wilder and North America Syndicate

managers working for the Army were charged and convicted for illegally disposing of chemical waste. The rules of the management game have changed; leaders can no longer hide under the skirt of corporate or federal immunity. Managers can be convicted because they "should have known" and "had the power . . . to prevent the violation and knowingly failed to prevent, detect, or correct the violation." The Department of Justice is starting at the bottom and going as high as possible in finding managers that failed to act to handle violations *and* failed to communicate the problem up the organization. If you know there is a problem, deal with it before it deals with you.

We are not talking civil action here. We are seeing the extension of criminal statutes to the workplace. Legal precedents are being established for future prosecutions of managers who fail to confront problems that might be caused by the negligence of people responsible to them.

In none of these cases will managers be able to hide behind Chapter 11 proceedings. The message is clear: you can avoid confronting people who are not doing their jobs, and you can also pay hefty fines and go to jail.

"No discipline without pain."

—Havelock Ellis

Okay already, you're probably thinking by now: I get the point. He's told me in about fifteen different ways that I've got to be a hardnosed SOB or I'm a lousy manager. There's no room for caring and understanding when you're managing people; it's dog-eat-dog. It's a jungle out there. . . . Forget all this team and empowerment garbage; real leaders still know how to motivate. Get rid of the bums!

If that's the message you've derived from this chapter, read it again. Rest assured that you don't have to transform yourself into a modern day Simon Legree in order to be an effective leader. You do have to hold people accountable—*that's a manager's job!* Fortunately there are ways you can do this without sacrificing caring and understanding, as long as you don't confuse caring with reluctance to confront.

Keep an accurate record of the employee's on-the-job performance.

Most organizations follow a course of progressive constructive discipline. Work with your own manager and your organization's personnel department to be sure you're following your organization's guidelines. Don't wait till you have to use them. Be familiar with your discipline options.

For the first confrontation with a problem employee, most companies suggest an oral reprimand and a warning as an appropriate first step. Each subsequent time an employee is counseled, however, formal documentation is required for each interview. Most company forms require managers to specify incidents of ineffective performance or rule violation, identify appropriate expectations for the employee, and list any action taken. You may have to overcome a strong aversion to paperwork, but you will find that it is well worth the effort. In many cases, the employee's knowledge that a written record exists will be all the incentive she needs to get her act together. If the problem does persist, you have evidence of previous counseling; no one can say you didn't warn her. If eventually you come to see termination as the only solution to the problem, you will have a record of repeated instances of confrontation and discipline.

Help the employee to find a more suitable position.

You will often find that an employee's problems on the job relate to his being trapped in the wrong position. Why do they stay? The answer is simple; they feel they have no options. They can't afford to quit. They are afraid they'd lose their medical benefits and their pension. There'd be no money for the mortgage or for their kids' college tuition payments. They are haunted by fears—what if they couldn't find another job? Victims are hard to motivate. When workers feel trapped, they hold on for dear life, even to jobs they hate. In fact, if they are too tough for you to deal with, maybe you will leave them alone long enough for them to coast into retirement.

Don't throw in the towel yet. There may be appropriate lateral placements within the organization. Such a placement can work if the employee is motivated to make it work out, and if the manager does not perceive "transfer" as a euphemism for "dumping." Many "can'ts" are really "won'ts." You know this for a fact if you've ever noticed the way "good old Charlie's" performance suddenly improves the day the chairman of the board or district supervisor shows up to observe him as a typical employee! If you feel that motivation, not incompetence, is the problem, suggest a talk with the personnel manager. Appropriate counseling might help the employee determine whether he would be better suited to, and motivated by, a different position.

Another option is the "decision-making leave." This step should be taken if repeated, documented incidents have brought the employee to the brink of termination. Confront the employee once again, discuss the problem, and inform him that he is not to report to work the next day. Some companies pay the employee for the day. The decision-making leave is not meant as punishment but for considering options. The employee is to spend the day deciding whether to continue working for the organization and is to report his decision for the next day. Often this lays the groundwork for the employee's choice to leave for a more motivational job or for an appropriate lateral move.

In today's business environment, in which many people are being laid off for reasons other than poor performance, companies often provide out-placement services to help terminated employees find other positions. The caring manager will consider such alternatives whenever it is determined that the employee is trapped in the wrong position. If your organization is large enough to allow for such latitude, and if the employee's job classification is not bound by civil service or certification restrictions, such action could spare both you and the employee the unpleasantness of termination.

Do not forget that the caring manager who confronts and challenges her employees is not always liked. The manager who tries to balance understanding with accountability must expect frustration and disappointment as necessary, if temporary, by-products. A problem faced by most "nice" managers is that they need to be liked, and vocal complainers can shake their administrative resolve. But managers with a high need for affiliation, a need for the constant approval of their workers, seldom make good bosses. They tend to make exceptions for the negative and vocal few at the expense of the hard-working many. This is yet another example of what happens when a manager bends the rules for the difficult people. Her inconsistency conveys the message that what pays off is not work, but complaints. In her attempt to be liked, such a leader, not unlike that conciliatory basketball referee, ends up losing the respect of all on the team.

CARE ENOUGH TO CONFRONT **43**

"If you can't answer a man's argument, all is not lost; you can still call him vile names."

—Elbert Hubbard

There are times when you must say no. There are times when you must make unpopular decisions. But at all times, you also have the opportunity and the responsibility to listen, give recognition, and give support to your people. Just be sure that you care enough to tell them when they're flying too low. Care enough to confront—it's the only way you can be sure that you'll both land safely.

QUESTIONS WORTH ASKING

"What do you do when you have to confront a friend who works for you?"

Nowhere is consistency more important than in dealing with a friend, or with an individual who was once your organizational colleague but now works for you. Nothing can eat away at morale within a team more quickly than evidence that the boss is playing favorites. Do not confuse caring for a friend with timidity about being direct. If it's a friend who's causing the problem, consider how her colleagues will regard her if you fail to take the same action you would with anyone else. Whenever you manage a friend, keep that friendship an asset by having an early conversation. Before any problems arise, try saying, "I don't want our friendship to interfere with our ability to work together. I hope that if either of us has issues we need to address we won't hesitate to come to each other and discuss them."

"If I have to fire someone, how do I avoid feeling guilty about it?"

Don't think of yourself as a monster. If you informed the employee early and consistently of his shortcomings, he fired himself by not acting responsibly. If after the termination interview you begin to have feelings of guilt, review your documentation of the former employee's work record. Do not second-guess yourself. Feel satisfied that you made the right decision. Be up-front with the rest of your employees. Emphasize that the fired person's work record was the reason for her dismissal; that it had nothing to do with their own job security. Avoid disparaging personal remarks about the subordinate. They are not relevant, they are demeaning to you as a manager, and they could get you sued. You can still be hard on issues and soft on people.

KEEPERS

☐ Care enough to confront.

☐ Document to inform, not to punish.

☐ Know your eight thousand-foot level and hold your team to it.

☐ Be tough as nails *and* supportive.

☐ Be consistent: Be a vending machine, not a slot machine.

CHAPTER FIVE

Avoiding Avoidance:
Be a Problem Solver
Not a Problem Evader

"A good manager doesn't try and eliminate conflict; he tries to keep it from wasting the energies of his people. If you're the boss, and your people fight you openly when they think you are wrong—that's healthy. If they fight each other openly in your presence for what they believe in—that's healthy. But keep all the conflict eyeball to eyeball."

—Robert Townsend

Let's suppose you have someone in your organization who's been giving you a lot of headaches; let's call her Bertha. You've been reluctant to confront her before now; maybe that's the very reason you bought this book. Having read this far, you've decided to "care enough to confront." Maybe you've even made an entry in your desk calendar for next Monday: "Bertha dies!" But with Monday comes a pile of messages, the weekend mail, the usual beginning-of-the-week "must-do" list. You glance at your calendar and read your entry about Bertha, and an all-to-familiar uneasiness starts rising within you. "I'll get to it as soon as I get these vital things out of the way," you tell yourself. After all, you've waited all year to confront Bertha. What's an hour or two longer? You close your calendar and start in on the paperwork.

Welcome to the world of avoidance.

As with the caring-and-understanding trap, our avoidance of conflict has its roots in childhood. Most of us were programmed to avoid it wherever possible. Remember: "Don't make waves," "Don't rock the boat," "If I had wanted your opinion, I'd have given it to you," "Don't talk back to your mother!"? The message was clear. By adolescence, most of us had it solidly incorporated into our behavior patterns. We hated to disappoint our friends; we also had a hard time speaking up to authority figures.

Now we're adults with leadership responsibilities, but many of us still have the old avoidance tapes playing in our heads. As we face the prospect of conflict, we experience discomfort; the nearer the confrontation looms, the more the discomfort builds into full-fledged anxiety. As one manager confided before approaching his boss about a budget problem, "My stomach doesn't have butterflies; it's been invaded by eagles!"

A recent case study of a manager in precisely that situation documents the avoidance anxiety most graphically. As part of a stress study, this executive's blood pressure was taken at various intervals on the job. On the morning that he was due to confront his boss about a budget problem, his blood pressure was taken clinically and recorded at a quite reasonable 130/70. When he returned from the clinic, just thinking about his boss had raised his blood pressure to 150/90. After writing down his arguments in preparation for the meeting, it had risen to 160/90. Just before he went in to talk to the boss, it was all the way up to 186/129—the guy could have popped a cork! By lunch time, the meeting now behind him, the man's blood pressure was back to 130/70.

The anticipation of conflict activates the standard alarm reaction: the blood pressure mounts, the heartbeat accelerating as blood rushes to the extremities and the brain. This reaction may have served our prehistoric ancestors well in preparing them to fight saber-toothed cats, but it is not very constructive for a manager preparing to confront her boss.

Reprinted by permission of United Feature Syndicate, Inc.

But don't worry, your brain will come to the rescue. It has developed a vast repertoire of rationalizations to help you escape from the confrontation.

The closer you get to the meeting that's causing all the anxieties, the more reasons you find why "this is not the right time." Your thoughts might include any of the following: "She doesn't look like she wants to talk." "He hasn't eaten yet; he's an animal before he eats." "I don't want to ruin her day; maybe I should wait until just before she leaves."

"Maybe I should wait till Friday; I've heard it's better to confront before the weekend." "I don't think this is really that important; I'm probably making a mountain out of a molehill." "In a minute; I'll do it, but I've got to go to the bathroom first." By the time you come out of the restroom, Bertha is gone for the day.

With escape comes immediate relief. By avoiding the confrontation, we experience an immediate drop in subjective discomfort. "How do you spell RELIEF?" Escape Bertha! Soon, however, we are left with discomfort of a different sort: the renewed frustration of the unresolved problem and the guilt associated with avoidance. After reading this chapter, you'll probably feel even more guilt: "He told me I was going to do this, and sure enough, I'm doing it!" Whip-whip-whip-whip-whip . . . .

Even though most of us are good at guilt (we love wallowing in it), it's a backbreaker. And so we renew our commitment to confront the problem. "Tomorrow," we tell ourselves, and we make a note on our calendar. But tomorrow we find ourselves playing the same game all over again. People can go on like this for days. And the self-whipping continues. "My God, I can't believe this! I am in charge of this department! I'm the one who's supposed to take care of this! This is ridiculous! Why am I scared of Bertha? She's only a person!"

Whip-whip-whip-whip-whip. . . .

The built-up frustration of the avoidance trap contributes to on-the-job stress, inconsistent management, and time lost for problem solving. Many managers will take out their frustration on themselves through sleepless nights and stress-related illnesses. Others take it out on the nearest available scapegoats, such as a spouse, children, pets, passing motorists, or "resident dumpees" at work (clerks, secretaries, trainees, and nonassertive team members). Either way, it is costly, both to those we love and to those we manage.

Often we break out of the avoidance trap only when pressured by either of two naturally occurring events: we wait for deadlines, or we throw a managerial temper tantrum. Either one can cause our bags to be sent to Japan. In our deadline-oriented world, failure to confront a problem will increase the pressure. If you don't confront Bertha, you can't meet your deadline. Sometimes your boss helps you along. She finds you in the hallway and reminds you, "Hey, Jim. Have you talked to Bertha yet about the Payne account?" Your apologetic reply identifies the problem: "No, I haven't had a chance to. I'll get on it today."

Now you have an added motivation—fear! That is usually the push you need to force yourself into action. But now you no longer have any choice about when to confront Bertha. By waiting for the pressure of a

deadline, you have been forced to become one of those all-too-preva-
lent "crisis managers." Now when you confront Bertha, there will be little time for considered action. This means that the confrontation
you've been avoiding is far more likely to be negative. The Berthas of
this world rarely react positively to crisis problem solving.

And when the confrontation goes poorly, you'll be even more likely
to evade the next one: "What a nightmare that was! Next time I'm going
to avoid confronting her until I have to!" And so the cycle begins again:
avoidance-guilt-avoidance-guilt-crisis-conflict-avoidance. The procrastinators of the world are rarely the initiators; they are dependent on others for the push needed to get the job done. We become procrastinators;
no "amateur crastinators" are we. Procrastinating managers "crastin-
ate" and get paid for it.

If deadlines won't force you to act, you can always wait until your
anger does the job for you. Resentment is often a by-product of avoidance. We say to ourselves, "I shouldn't even have to say this. She should
know she's not doing her job! It should be perfectly obvious!" We stay
enmeshed in the avoidance trap until our anger catapults us out: It
doesn't bother me, it doesn't bother me, it doesn't bother me, it doesn't
bother me—it bothers me! BERTHA DIES! You ride the trajectory of
anger out of your office, down the hall and into Bertha's office: "I told
you to get that order in a month ago! You get that on my desk this afternoon, or you're gone! Is that clear enough for you?"

Bertha's silent stare tells you all you need to know. You turn and leave
her office as quickly as you came in.

Anger can generate the force you need to break through your anxiety.
But as you've probably noticed, most people don't make a lot of sense
when they're angry. Anger is a low-brain function. It's sub-cortical;
there's no data down there. About the only thing it's good for is name-
calling. When we are angry we are seldom good listeners. We don't want
to listen; we want to pound it into them. How many times have you
emptied both barrels at someone before hearing them out? If we're
wrong, our anger only makes us look more foolish. We don't actually
shoot managers or team members, but we sure feel like it when we wait
too long to act.

By descending to name-calling and abuse, we rarely set the stage for
cooperation. Such an aggressive confrontation may make us feel better,
but it seldom solves problems. Instead, it creates new ones. Bertha may
miss your message entirely and remember only your abusiveness. She'll
take care of the Payne account, all right, but she'll also be sending your

luggage to as many different locations as she can find. She'll also be telling everyone else in the department what a monster you are.

And how do you feel after you've been aggressive? Initially you may justify your behavior: "She deserved it. Bertha's defective!" But within an hour you're likely to feel that you blew it: "I did it again, I lost my temper!" (Whip-whip-whip-whip-whip. . .) You're back wallowing in guilt. The result is understandable. You want to apologize. If you're one of those people who can't apologize, you lay low for awhile.

And the next time the problem comes up, the avoidance trap is that much stickier. You don't want to blow it again, do you? Avoidance-guilt-avoidance-resentment-avoidance-explosion-guilt-avoidance: the cycle continues.

"I won't think of it now. I can't stand it if I do. I'll think of it tomorrow. . . . Tomorrow is another day."

—"Scarlet O'Hara"

Effective leaders must learn to avoid avoidance; to be problem solvers, not problem evaders. Try the following strategies to help you break out of the avoidance trap.

Don't procrastinate.

There's no arcane mystery to why we procrastinate; it's simply a psychological ploy we use to stay within our comfort zones. We procrastinate, waiting for the right time; and then, when external pressures drag us kicking and screaming out of our comfort zones, we react. We may get the job done, but the cost can be high. Keep in mind that if you wait until pressure forces you to act, you are not in control of your time. You are letting events control you.

"What the hell—you might be right, and you might be wrong. . . but just don't avoid."

—Katherine Hepburn

A good rule to follow is to allow yourself a firm time limit for confronting a problem person. Three days is a reasonable cutoff time. If you haven't found a "right time" within three days, make time. This forces you to keep problem solving current.

Conflict does produce anxiety. No book is going to alter that fact. Keep in mind, however, that most anxiety is anticipatory. Recognize that once the confrontation is under way, your anxiety level will drop in response to the orienting process of your brain. The critical stimulation involved in talking, listening, and thinking will ease your discomfort. Once you realize that a confrontation is necessary, try some of these statements on yourself to get you past the initial anxiety:

"I'll feel better when this is done."

"The earlier we face a problem, the easier it is to fix."

"Hidden problems become big problems."

"If I do this early, it will start my day off on a positive roll."

"I'm not trying to inflict pain; I'm trying to make a necessary course correction."

"It may be nothing; find out early."

"Do it now! Waiting only wastes time and makes things worse!"

"I'm a problem solver, not a problem evader."

HERMAN®

"Have a good vacation. I've decided not to give you your bad news until you get back."

Then seek out your "Bertha" and solve the problem. Early problem solving becomes a habit that can break the cycle of avoidance.

Make an appointment to solve the problem.

Making an appointment with the problem individual is an excellent way of breaking the avoidance cycle. It divides the anxiety-producing action into two steps: making the appointment and holding the interview. It also ensures that you will follow through. If Bertha is expecting an appointment, it's unlikely that you'll duck out with, "Oh, I, uh, I just wanted to say "Hi. How are the kids?" Commitment increases the probability of action. You might also want to tell a colleague or your secretary about the upcoming appointment to increase your likelihood of action.

The more difficult or defensive the person can be, the more important an appointment is. It increases the likelihood that you and she will be prepared for problem solving, not for war. One of the most difficult aspects of conflict is the element of surprise. It's an important advantage in a military situation, but not in a confrontation you hope to keep constructive. When surprised, many people react defensively: "It's not my problem!" or with a counterattack: "Well, you're not so hot either, turkey!" These are reflex reactions, and neither of them is helpful in solving problems. By making the appointment, you allow both of you the opportunity to prepare.

Never make the appointment without establishing what the agenda will be. If you tell Bertha you want to see her at three, but you don't tell her why, it'll waste her whole day. She'll think of everything she's done wrong since she started working for you, and she'll be readying her weapons for a counteroffensive. If instead you tell her, "I've been thinking about that problem we've been having about the Payne account. I'd like to take ten minutes of your time this afternoon to discuss what we might do about it," you have set the stage for problem solving, not fault-finding. Indeed, Bertha might have the problem solved before the appointment. With any luck, you may have the option of using your eyes and ears instead of your mouth. It could also save you the embarrassment of making suggestions about how to solve the problem when she's got a better one.

Other managers break out of the avoidance cycle by scheduling frequent one-on-one sessions with their boss and with their subordinates. A weekly commitment of fifteen to twenty minutes may be all it takes to keep problem solving current. At these meetings, "red-flag" potential problems by requesting that they be brought up first. This brings conflicts to the surface before they can become major problems that affect staff morale. Holding regular appointments also puts to rest the notions that every appointment with the boss means bad news. The one-on-one sessions will provide you with opportunities for listening, prioritizing projects, and supporting your workers. But they can provide regular and timely occasions for confronting problems as well.

Visualize a successful confrontation.

Every confrontation can be seen as an opportunity to assist, rather than to win over, the other party. While Bertha is preparing herself for the appointment, use your time to visualize a positive discussion focused on future successes, not past problems. Get a clear mental image of your anxiety level dropping as you discuss the possible solutions. Visualize a smile forming on your face as you greet her and ask her to take a seat. Visualize yourself listening intently to her ideas and leaving with a mutually agreeable solution. By visualizing success you build success. When Bertha steps into your office at three o'clock, you'll be ready for problem solving, not World War III.

Make problem solving a priority.

This brings us back to procrastination. It's all too easy to hide behind paper, meetings, and unimportant details while you avoid the "people problems" that are keeping you and others from getting your jobs done. Think about this the next time you shuffle that "Talk to Bertha" message to the bottom of your in-box while you devote your attention to a list of trivialities. Keeping a "to-do" list is good common-sense time management, but it doesn't go far enough. There is something innately satisfying about crossing items off a list. By mid-afternoon, you may have crossed off twelve or sixteen items. You'll be feeling superficially pleased with yourself, but you'll still go home full of frustration if one of the items remaining is "Talk to Bertha."

By prioritizing the tasks at hand, you make it easier to recognize when you're playing "trivial pursuit." You make it harder to rationalize your avoidance. Make "Talk to Bertha" a top priority; then do it early in the day. The rest of the day will all seem downhill from there: "I did it! I confronted Bertha and I survived!" You'll have created your own momentum.

The difference between assertive and aggressive behavior is often nothing more than a matter of timing. Deal promptly with impending conflict and you have the option of being assertive and constructive. Procrastinate, and your frustration and anxiety build up like pressure in a steam boiler. By the time the inevitable confrontation takes place, you're boiling mad. All you're left with is your anger. You pass on your anxiety to the other guy. And while he may then scurry about in a conspicuous effort to make you happy, he's also going to be finding every conceivable way to send your bags to Japan.

Learn to avoid avoidance. Anticipate the discomfort that comes with conflict, but push through it to reap the benefits of timely problem solving. Deal assertively with conflict instead of removing all options but the executive tantrum. Become a problem solver, not a problem evader.

QUESTIONS WORTH ASKING

"Aren't there times when it's wise to avoid confrontations?"

Yes! There is appropriate withdrawal. If you are angry, and you know you won't handle a confrontation effectively, the responsible thing to do is to keep your distance. You don't want your emotions to control the encounter; you want to solve problems, not create new ones. It's the old count-to-ten strategy. Take time to focus your message, but don't let a responsible distance become a long-standing avoidance. Talking to a colleague or writing down your concern will help you focus your message. Once you're in control, do not hesitate to confront the problem. You'll be ready to deal with it effectively, not emotionally.

KEEPERS

☐ Avoid avoidance: be a problem solver, not a problem evader.

☐ Set a time limit; then confront.

☐ Make appointments for confronting your difficult people.

☐ Make problem solving a priority by putting your calendar where your mouth is.

☐ Keep problem solving focused on the future.

☐ Visualize a positive outcome to your problem-solving efforts.

CHAPTER SIX

Building Bridges vs. Burning Them: The Subtle Art of Influence

"The major reason capable people fail to advance is that they don't work well with their colleagues. The statement, 'He's good, but he has trouble getting along with other people,' is the kiss of death for management potential. . . . The key to success is not information. It's people."

—Lee Iacocca

So far we've been hammering away at a manager's need to confront. We have learned that timely confrontations are necessary for ensuring accountability and for solving problems. But if a workplace relationship is defined by confrontation, serious problems result. The people involved become locked in an ongoing series of negative interactions. Instead of listening to each other, they grab for their new weapons (one-upmanship, flanking maneuvers, documentation, malicious gossip, dirty tricks) and prepare for battle. Their polarization crowds out any possibility of constructive conflict. It is costly, both to the individuals and to the organization that provides the arena for battle, since both parties are expending time and energy sending each other's bags to Japan.

This chapter is about how successful managers find that elusive winning balance—the balance, as Peters put it, between being supportive and being tough as nails.

In leadership, as in statecraft, a critical component in managing conflict is building diplomatic bridges to even your worst adversary. Unfortunately, the art of persuasion is far more subtle than the art of

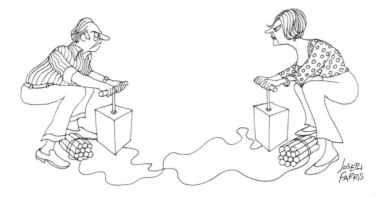

confrontation. Bridges can easily be burned amid the din of battle. Then, instead of building a new bridge, we put up walls.

Intuitively, we know the value of bridge building in influencing others. Relationships are like bank-deposit systems. When you write checks on your account, they will be honored only as long as there are deposits to cover them. Similarly, in our interpersonal accounts, we want to be sure we have sufficient positive interactions on deposit.

We "touch" people in many ways, and it pays off. We are more likely to go to bat for friends and valued associates with whom we have a history of reciprocity. That history helps to set the stage for caring and mutual respect. We know that this is "how to win friends and influence people." But when push comes to shove in our busy world, we often substitute crisis-contact for diplomacy. Instead of bridging the wall of conflict, we try to burn it down.

And then the battle line is drawn; the enemy is before us. We find ourselves in a polarized relationship without realizing how we got there. Often it begins early in the relationship, before the individuals involved have had an opportunity to develop any history of positive interaction. The battle may be touched off by an actual or anticipated negative experience; by physical or emotional distance from the other party; by a well-intentioned warning or criticism; by our own biases; sometimes by a touch of projection. The enemy could be a peer, a team member, a boss, or a customer. But the result of these wars tends always to be the same—everyone loses. They sap the energy and time of managers in every sort of business or institution.

"One man cannot hold another man down in the ditch
without remaining down in the ditch with him."

—Booker T. Washington

The easiest thing to do is to blame the other party. We know that he "should" listen to authority; she "should work more cooperatively"; they "should" be more supportive. Yet as much as "they" seem to enjoy the battle, most people truly would rather cooperate with others on the job. Before we pass the blame for striking the match, we ought to have a clear picture of how we ourselves often pour the gasoline.

Ron had just been named superintendent of Tinker Construction Company. Before he took charge, the man he was replacing warned him about his subcontractor: "Look out for Bill; he's a real animal!" Before he even had a chance to meet Bill, he was given similar warnings by other colleagues: "That man will eat you alive! I can't believe they gave you this job!" On checking the company records, Ron discovered that because of a lack of supervision by previous superintendents, Bill had often failed to have his men do the finishing work on completed homes. Ron knew he would have to confront Bill. As all bets were on Bill, and people weren't afraid to let him know it, Ron was resigned to a major ordeal. He called Bill in and took a firm stand on refusing to authorize any new building starts until the finishing work was done. Bill laughed sarcastically and snarled: "Do you realize how many houses we're supposed to build this month? How long have you been in this business anyway?" As he stalked out, he hurled his clipboard across the room.

*　　*　　*　　*　　*　　*

Though Marcia was still in her twenties, she had established herself as a progressive district manager for Sunshine Unlimited, a growing investment company. She enjoyed good relations with most of her branch managers, but two in particular had resisted her leadership. Both were long-time company men who resented reporting to someone they viewed as a "token woman." After sending a procedural memo to all branch managers requiring a change in monthly account-tracking procedures, she was confronted in her office by Harry, one of the malcontents. "I knew this would happen when they put you in this position!" he shouted, throwing a copy of the memo down on her desk. "I suggest you put this up on your wall, because seven years from now, when you grow up, you're going to realize what you've done!" Before she could respond, he turned and left the room.

*   *   *   *   *   *

Sig was sales manager for Byte Brothers Software, Inc. Ever since he had started with the company, he had had a difficult time working with Mel, the manager of the design department. The tension, exacerbated by mutual animosity and resentment between the two departments, often erupted into full-scale warfare. One morning, a saleswoman came into Sig's office, threw a file down on his desk, and said, "I can't believe this guy. If we don't meet this deadline for the Shredlu account, we've as good as lost it! He could get it done in time, but he won't!" Sig picked up the phone, but Mel's answer was predictable: "It's always urgent with you guys," he yawned. "We'll do the best we can." The best was not enough: Byte Brothers lost the account.

In each of these cases, you've probably made a determination as to which party is "wrong." What must be realized is that being "right" or "wrong" may be of little consequence in solving the problem. In none of these situations is anyone's competence in question. Ron needs Bill to get his houses built. Marcia recognizes that Harry, sexist though he may be, is a shrewd trader with some valuable accounts. And Sig, in his heart of hearts, knows that Mel's package designs help to sell software. In all these cases, people's personal animosities prevent them from working together. The only basis on which the two individuals have learned to relate to one another is negative. It is such private warfare that makes positive, constructive, problem solving difficult.

Sig and Mel, to take an example, are each convinced that the other is "out to get him." They head separate departments; they keep their distance and interact only to the extent that business demands it. At such a distance, each begins selectively to scan the other for evidence to support his distrust. When something positive does occur (Mel's department produces a promised design before Sig's sales reps start to get angry, or Sig expresses some understanding of the time required for the creative process) they seldom are willing to appreciate or to trust it. Both have been known to say: "Well, it's about time, but it won't last!" "He's up to something. What is he after?" All it takes is a frown across the cafeteria to trigger visions of an assassination plot. It may only be indigestion, but it will be interpreted as hate. Neither party initiates positive interaction; neither feels that it would do any good. Both are convinced that the other can never change.

The same sort of strain can be kicked off by the mere anticipation of a problem. Before Ron had even met Bill, others had painted a picture of the subcontractor as "the animal." He expected to have problems with Bill, and so he did. The anticipated conflict and selective scanning triggered the very problem he feared.

As for Harry and Marcia, our prejudices can set the stage for similar problems. Before you hang the pig's snout on Harry's face, consider the biases you have had to overcome. You may quite reasonably be outraged at the notion that "women don't belong in management," but try some of these on for size: men are all chauvinists; blacks are lazy; whites are racists; old people are slow, inefficient, and set in their ways; young people are undedicated and self-absorbed. If any of these statements fit you, even to a small degree, you have set the stage for destroying a potential work relationship. Oh, but you couldn't be so crass as to allow sexism, racism, or ageism to compromise your working relationships? Then how about these: accountants are all bean counters; computer programmers are circuit heads; psychologists are nutty as fruitcakes; auditors are the ones who go in after the battle to shoot the wounded. Each of us has biases that create distance and the anticipation of problems. It is part of your job as a leader to recognize your biases and to work to overcome their influence.

> *"Love your enemies, bless them that curse you, do good to*
> *them that hate you, and pray for them which despitefully use*
> *you and persecute you."*
>
> —Matthew 5:44

It is necessary. Either you improve the relationship or your bags are on the way to new and exciting locations. Outside of work we can usually pick the people we want to enjoy our time with. We can stay in our comfort zones. On the job, we can't always count on it. A great many of the people we have to work with may be people we'd rather not even see. But since you have to work with them, you must find a way to minimize the animosity. Bridge building can be a matter of overcoming our own prejudices, but it can also be a matter of laying a foundation for the other guy to overcome his.

> *"My most important contribution to IBM was my ability to*
> *pick strong and intelligent men and then hold them together*
> *by persuasion, by apologies, by financial incentives, by*
> *speeches, by chatting with their wives, by thoughtfulness when*
> *they were sick or involved in accidents, and using every tool at*
> *my command to make that team think that I was a decent*

guy. I knew I couldn't match all of them intellectually, but I thought that, if I used fully every capacity I had, I could stay even with them.

I never hesitated to promote someone I didn't like. The comfortable assistant, the nice guy you like to go on fishing trips with, is a great pitfall. Instead I looked for those sharp, scratchy, harsh, almost unpleasant guys who see and tell you about things as they really are. If you can get enough of them around you and have patience enough to hear them out, there is no limit to where you can go."

—Thomas Watson, Jr., Former IBM CEO

With that kind of attitude, you can understand how Thomas Watson Jr. helped keep the IBM giant dancing at the top of the Fortune 500 charts. He knew how to keep potential "enemies" working together as a productive team.

Once again let us be reminded that ultimately, the only person we influence is ourselves. Building bridges to our workplace "enemies" is a matter of changing our own behavior. You cannot make another person like you, nor do you need to. You don't even need her approval. But you do need to work with her. For that to happen successfully, you need to make it difficult for her to continue to perceive you as an enemy.

"I don't like that man. I'm going to have to get to know him better."

—Abraham Lincoln

It is difficult to initiate bridge building when a relationship is colored by bias or by a long history of negative interaction. In such cases, you may feel that giving your adversary any recognition or support would be insincere. But consider how your own behavior might be contributing to the problem. You may be scanning her selectively for aspects of her personality that support your dislike. Don't be insincere; look for ways to be sincere. Use your scanner to look for attributes that will support positive contact. If you can give a sincere compliment to a friend, is it hypocritical to compliment an adversary for a similar accomplishment or contribution? If you look for such opportunities and take them, you may find that positive feelings, yours and hers, will follow.

But maybe you've tried. Maybe you feel that your particular "Bertha" or "Charlie" is unique: "I try to meet him halfway, but it doesn't do any good." Consider what you'd be thinking if he tried to build a bridge to

HERMAN®

7-26

**"D'you wanna tip me now?
Then I'll know what sort
of service to give you."**

you: "He's up to something! He's probably just come back from another seminar. It won't last long!" If you owed ten thousand dollars, few banks would be overjoyed to receive your first $100 payment.

It takes a history of positive contact to build trust in a polarized relationship. Most of us are willing to "try" being positive, but few of us ever follow through consistently. Only continued bridge building will give the relationship a chance to improve. Give the bridge-building process the time you need to make it work. Even if it doesn't work, don't be a manager that just "tries" something. "Be" something. By making a consistent stand as a positive bridge builder to all you work with, you build a reputation all will see and come to respect even if a few never respond.

Again we must emphasize the need for balance. You may be thinking, "If I try to build bridges to Charlie; if I compliment him and play 'nice, nice' all the time, he'll see it as a sign of weakness. All that hardnose understands is strength." If you continue to confront him strongly whenever such action is appropriate, you won't be taken advantage of when you build your bridges. Conversely, if you take every appropriate opportunity to build a bridge, you'll find that the confrontations, when they become necessary, will be more positive and more easily directed toward problem solving. Both are important; neither stands alone effectively in our changing world.

*"Politicians don't talk about wielding power. That's so crass.
The only thing I hope is that I will continue to be able to
influence by. . . persuasion . . . nothing heavy handed. Just
openness and good relations."*

—Barbara Jordan

Let's look at some of the tools and techniques that are available to us for building positive influence and rapport. The following suggestions by no means exhaust the possibilities, but they will give you an idea of the breadth of the options available to you for bridge building. Keep in mind that every action suggested here is probably something you already do with the people you respect and with whom you work well. The trick is to get out of your comfort zone and extend your bridge building to your "Berthas" and "Charlies" as well.

Get to know all the people you need to influence.

Our tendency to distance difficult people is, in part, simply a matter of habit based on personal preference. Most of us find our individuals of choice within our first month on the job. We have lunch with them, take our breaks in their offices, socialize with them after work; and if conflict arises with them, we usually have no trouble working things out. But the people who are left out can easily confuse such a natural personal preference for favoritism, even though they themselves might have formed similar relationships with their own people of preference.

Building bridges does not require you to invite your adversaries to go bowling, just to make yourself less distant. Take another look at ways to build a new positive history. If Sig takes the trouble to tell Mel how favorably the retailers are reacting to the new packaging concepts, it could be the first step toward a genuine peace treaty. If Ron resists his natural inclination to distance himself from Bill, he might discover that "the animal" has some useful ideas. If he frequently uses and clearly appreciates Bill's input, some Monday morning he might find to his surprise that the houses targeted for finishing work that week have already been completed. And if Marcia can resist seeing the snout and the curly tail every time she thinks of Harry (if she doesn't distance herself from him because of his attitude), eventually he's going to recognize her competence. Let's face it, she's probably never going to turn the guy into an activist for the Women's Movement. About the best she can hope for is an assessment like, "Yeah, I've got to admit, she runs this department like a man." But that may be all she needs to work effectively with him. Biases take time to change, but people can overcome them.

Such an accommodation was made by a teacher I met on a plane not long ago. She had left teaching when her husband's career had forced a move, but was compelled to go back to work when he became a casualty of wholesale layoffs in the automobile industry. The only position she could find was at a tough high school in inner-city Detroit. She was replacing a teacher who had suffered a nervous breakdown after six weeks in the classroom. This woman was about four feet, ten inches tall, and white.

Going in with the awareness that there were likely to be discipline problems and that no one was going to be physically intimidated by her, she tried a strategy that had always worked for her in the past. Any time she disciplined a student, she would find a way to initiate positive contact as well. She would put a hand on a student's shoulder while helping him; she would talk cordially to them during passing periods. At lunchtime she ate with students more often than with teachers; she went to football games and sat with the difficult students. And the kids loved her. They were loyal to her and they worked with her. At the end of her "rookie year" she was voted the school's best teacher. We need teachers like that. We need leaders that will go beyond position power to develop people power. ·

Small talk can be better than no talk at all.

At best, our interactions with our workplace adversaries are characterized by polite indifference. Break the pattern by practicing what Peters and Waterman popularized as MBWA—Management by Wandering Around. Learn to master the art of timely small talk. Seek out occasions for informal conversations with your "problem person." Blow the beast's mind; sit next to him at meetings; make a point of catching him at the water cooler; walk with him to the parking lot at the end of the day; pause to say more than just "Hi" when you pass him in the hallway. Listen for information about his interests, opinions, or activities to find some common ground. Use the free information you receive to direct your questions and to focus your own self-disclosures. Share of yourself: your values, hobbies, activities, and interests.

If people are truly your "most important resource," you can't afford not making yourself accessible to them. Some successful companies suggest that up to thirty percent of a manager's time be spent on such visibility functions. Certainly you have days when you do have time, there is no excuse for not getting out of your office and into contact with people. Building common ground through small talk should never take a large amount of time; it's not necessary to become a "professional visitor." You have a job to do, but a small investment in cordiality can often pay healthy dividends in cooperation.

Don't be afraid of using your computer to keep track of your professional network, just as a sales representative would keep track of his clients. One well meaning manager, using his contact management database, disciplined himself to list five common ground areas he had with each person in his influence network. He'd review his files frequently, sending cards on appropriate occasions. He'd seek out and sit with his difficult people before meetings and explore "safe" conversations where the rapport could build. Not only did it build a bridge, it gave him a chance to get to know his "enemy."

One top-level executive at a large computer firm told me that his particular bridge-building strategy was to locate his office near the restrooms. "An executive corner office may give you a great view, but it doesn't give you the people contact you need," he said. By arranging to have an office near the restrooms, he was assured of seeing everyone he needed to influence at least two or three times a day. It also gave him a way of handling the long-winded ones: He'd catch them on the way in.

Join forces in a common cause.

Common interests can be the basis of common cause. This simple truth of group psychology is such a cliche that it's easy to ignore it. Its most classic expression is in the camaraderie of soldiers in combat. If you've never been one yourself, consider the stock-company "all-American" platoon of the war movies of the '40s: the quiet, oaken-hearted farm boy; the brash, crap-shooting Brooklyn wise guy; the introspective young black man; the hulking redneck with the chip on his shoulder; the bookish college man with a dream. Their mutual indifference and mistrust becomes inconsequential when the enemy's guns are pointing in their direction.

We're not suggesting a declaration of war against the company on the other side of the parking lot. There are less drastic means of developing rapport within your organization. Often we find ourselves in an emotional battle with an adversary whom we agree with on most of the important issues. When you can sincerely support a program or a position that an enemy is promoting, make your support a matter of record. Support the issue publicly, and offer your assistance privately. Find a task force or a committee that you can both work for, and stay actively involved. Focusing on such issues will help the two of you to develop a base of sincere cooperation on which to build a positive relationship.

And if there is no common ground for bridge building at work, why not try outside work? Sports clubs, associations, and other mutual interests can provide the structure for contact that can build positive responsiveness. Maybe you want to invite your adversary to play racquetball. Whether sports or hobbies provide the common ground, or whether you work together to coordinate a fashion show, a concert, or a charity fund-raiser, when you find the potential for a bridge, build it.

Remember this idea when you find yourself managing two people who don't get along with each other. In this situation most managers separate the two people and then allow factions to form, infecting the staff with dissension and eroding morale. The manager ends up in the middle, loathed by both sides. Try a different strategy. Find some cause that will make the two people allies and hold them accountable for working toward a common goal. More than one manager has spoken of the value of having two "enemies" work together. It gave them a common cause and a common enemy—their boss. They both had to work together to make something happen, and they both hated the boss for making them work together. "Not only did it warm up their relationship," one manager told me concerning this tactic, "I had more time to myself. Neither one of them wanted anything to do with me for a month. But it worked; they now work together as a team."

Don't be afraid to ask for input or help.

Don't laugh at this one. It is one thing to make demands in the heat of battle; it is quite another to ask for help when no conflict is involved. You might be surprised by the support you receive and by the bridge you build in the process.

"Get your enemies to read your works in order to mend them; for your friend is so much like your second self that he will judge too much like you."

—Alexander Pope

We often try to win people over by helping them. But if we help an adversary too much, we are sending an unwelcome message: "Sister, do you need help!" Enemies don't like to hear this message. There is certainly nothing wrong with helping people, but even friends can feel suffocated by too much assistance. As psychologist Erich Fromm theorizes in *Man for Himself*, the most difficult person to deal with is the person who is giving their all for us. We will repress any anger that we feel because we owe them so much. As time passes, our resentment of the unevenness of the situation causes our repressed anger to boil over.

If, on the other hand, we ask our adversary for input in their area of expertise, we send a message of respect. Don't try this if you don't respect the person's experience and knowledge in a particular area. Laughing at their suggestions or ignoring them will not build bridges.

Asking for input should not be restricted to your adversaries; it is a valuable strategy that can build a broad base of mutual support for ideas. It provides an organizational context for listening and participation. The chances of one individual's proposal being accepted within an organization are minimal at best. The interests of ego and bureaucracy usually assure that the idea will be drawn and quartered. But seeking input from all involved allows you to capitalize on the strengths of everyone within your network: your peers, superiors, subordinates and customers, in addition to your enemies. Learn their strengths, pick the right time and ask for help. Then the proposal isn't "mine"; it's "ours"— and it's well on its way to acceptance.

The same manager who kept five common interests in his computer database, forced himself to list five strengths each person had that were better than his own skills. When he needed help on any project, he'd go to his computer and it would quickly list the people who had the expertise requried. He would ask for their help, use much of their valuable input, and, as a result, secure their buy-in when their support was needed. He not only was a master bridge builder; his strategy always improved the quality of his team's work.

Give more than your share of credit and take more than your share of blame.

Asking an adversary for input will build no bridges if you fail subsequently to acknowledge his contribution. Giving credit where it is due is a good idea, whether you solicited the input or whether it grew out of the ordinary routine of the job. Be generous with recognition, private and public, no matter what your past history with the person may be. Don't waste any time deciding whether Charlie needs recognition; decide whether he deserves it. Then give it to him whether he needs it or not. The very person who seems not to need recognition may be the very one who keeps score of the number of times you recognize others, but ignore him. Don't trouble yourself about whether the tactic will "work"; ask yourself instead what kind of manager (and what kind of human being) you would like to be.

Never participate in negative gossip. No matter how big your organization might be, there is no guarantee that what you say won't get back to the person being gossiped about. Instead, learn the art of positive gos-

"I'm trying out a technique called 'positive reinforcement.' I'm supposed to catch you doing something right. So will you hurry up!"

sip. Make your recognition public as well as private. Be sure to let Charlie's colleagues know you appreciate what he's done. Then Charlie will hear "gossip" that goes something like, "Hey, Jill was talking about you. She said your contribution to the proposal is what clinched the deal." And all the while, Charlie figured Jill was taking the credit for his work and blaming him for her foul-ups! It's just plain hard for an enemy to handle.

> *"There is no limit to what you can accomplish if you don't care who gets the credit."*
> —Leslie G. McGraw, Jr., president of Fluor Corp.

If something has gone wrong, take more than your share of the blame yourself—and do it publicly. When you confront the guilty party, do it eyeball to eyeball—and in private. Your integrity will not go unnoticed.

Jim Jumbles had not had a good day in starting his third week in the data processing department for Vixon Visuals. He had lost key data from key accounts on the main terminal databank. He had

had hard copy but no backup. Expecting the worst, he went with his bad news to Edna Earling, his manager. In the midst of his explanation, the division manager, Ralph Ruff, exploded into the room in a rage. He had just been yelled at by the Chief of Operations and seemed to be enjoying passing the pain down hill. Jim watched for fifteen minutes as Edna was fried on the corporate grill for his mistake. She not once mentioned his name; she took all the heat. Before Ralph left, Edna presented a plan of action and a timetable for completion. Now left alone, Jim expected it to be his turn. Edna did not even look at him. She closed her eyes and took a deep breath. She smiled, turned to him and said, "Don't do that again." He all but died, running at the mouth in a stream of apologies and promises. She knew it had been a legitimate error on his part and had appreciated his reporting the error. She requested his help in turning the problem around; you can guess his repsonse. Jim did not make the same mistake again.

Give support where needed.

Customer service extends to "enemies." Never let your feelings about another co-worker or team member stop you from doing your job. The motivation to serve may, at times, seem forced and less than authentic, but the need to break the cycle of bags to Japan has to start somewhere. Even if the track record of the person has been less than impressive, find ways to meet their needs when your job provides the opportunity. Don't let your track record of performance be the fuel that ignites another round of revenge.

Be an information broker.

Sometimes bridge building has to be done over a physical distance; learn to use the mail. Information brokers know the needs and interests of people in their influence network, and they help meet those needs by sending targeted articles that inform. Many professionals have a hard time keeping up in their areas of expertise; in a changing world that can be dangerous. If you read articles that would be of interest to anyone you work with, make a copy, highlight a couple of key points, attach a business card with a note, "Thought you'd like to see this," and let your mailman build your bridge. Not only does it build a bridge, you're seen as a professional that keeps up with changes—and it gives you something to do with your stack of business cards.

Learn to keep it light.

Laughter, to paraphrase Victor Borge, can be the shortest distance between two people. It can be the surest way to dissipate tension and animosity. The sort of humor we're talking about here is warmer than joke-telling. It's finding something to laugh about in everyday events, even in situations where other people would be more likely to cry.

Hannah Hippie had been appointed to head the math department at Aurora High School, and from the first day she found herself embroiled in conflict with the principal over curriculum and class staffing. One morning there was a particularly heated argument, and Hannah left the room in great distress. Later that day, in a corridor, she saw the principal coming out of a doorway and to avoid him, she ducked inside the first available door. As she opened it, she realized it was a closet. But she had committed herself, and she had no time to think. She closed the door, and after waiting what seemed to be a judicious length of time, she opened it a crack and took a tentative step into the hall. The principal pulled the door open and said, "Hello. Do you like it in there?" Hannah literally grabbed her boss. "Don't you dare let anyone know I was in there!" she gasped. Then they both burst out laughing. From then on they both worked well together. Every time one would smile, the other would crack a grin too, thinking of their private joke.

Most of us are aware of the tranquilizing effect of laughter, but we tend to reserve our sense of humor for the people with whom we're comfortable. The others get only polite indifference. They are left with the feeling, "She laughs it up with them all the time, but never with me. Guess I'm just not part of the inner circle. Or maybe, maybe she's laughing at me!" Don't be afraid to bring humor to any of your work relationships. People like to work with people that make work fun and laughter can make work fun. Keep in mind that laughing at your enemies is no way to build bridges, but laughing at yourself may be. Be able to take your job seriously and yourself lightly. Laughter can contribute to a sense of teamwork and can do much for the office's collective temperament and morale.

Don't forget to smile.

Never confuse professionalism with chronic seriousness. You may not be the kind of person who feels comfortable using humor, but this shouldn't be a reason for presenting a constant appearance of pain and distress to those you work with. Don't leave your face in park. Failure to be cordial can get your bags sent to Japan.

> *"The key element in good business management is emotional attitude. Management is a living force; there must be a visible emotional commitment."*
> —Harold Geneen and Alvin Moscow

If we were friendly to everyone we met on the street, we might not get home. But if we carry around that same countenance on the job, people confuse it with arrogance, distance, anger, and disapproval. Your friends know that "this isn't you," but meanwhile you're keeping an enemy an enemy. Become known for your welcoming smile and have a cordial greeting for everyone you work with. It might be all you need to open a door that might otherwise remain closed.

The challenge of building bridges will pay off with more than increased impact. You will also find that you are enjoying yourself more on the job. Putting your energy into interpersonal battles is costly to all concerned. Thinking about revenge and worrying about how you're going to remain one-up on the other guy saps your effectiveness and wastes your time. Team building starts with bridge building; let bridge building start with you. The ideas we've suggested here should by no means exhaust your options. Find your own strategies and work them into your own managerial style.

Don't expect your efforts to build a bridge every time. But by initiating positive contact, you are at least doing your part to avoid burning one down.

QUESTIONS WORTH ASKING

"Aren't there some people that no amount of bridge building will change?"

Without question, bridge building is not a magic kiss that will turn every toad into a Prince Charming. Your most difficult people may never change. There are no guarantees in dealing with people. You are guaranteed, however, that if you do nothing, nothing positive will happen. Develop a strategy that will give you the best possible batting average. Remember that significant changes in an adversarial relationship require balanced interaction over time. You will need to continue to confront when necessary, but you'll also be balancing the conflict with positive contact: Keep in mind that your goal is not to turn your department into Mr. Roger's Neighborhood, only to establish a context for working together without warfare.

"Isn't bridge building really just manipulation, even if it is done in a positive way?"

"Manipulation" has a negative connotation. "Influence" is a more acceptable word for the same objective. Since we don't control others, we must seek to influence the behavior of others in a direct, balanced, and straightforward way. In fact, as we've mentioned before, there is only one way to influence others: by providing the context that invites change within the other individual. You can provide this context with enemies and potential enemies as well as with the people you enjoy and respect. Is it manipulation when you build bridges to the people you enjoy working with? Of course not. Extending the same bridges to all the people you work with is not being manipulative. It is just being fair.

KEEPERS

☐ Build bridges, not walls.

☐ Relationships are like deposit systems: put something in before you try to take something out.

☐ Scan for ways to build sincere positive contacts.

☐ Trust comes from a history of balanced interaction.

☐ If you don't like someone, get to know her better.

☐ You don't have to be liked, but make yourself hard to be perceived as an enemy.

☐ Move beyond your biases and you'll find that people are people.

☐ Don't just try to build bridges, be a bridge builder for as long as it takes.

CHAPTER SEVEN

No Surprises: Using Future-Focused Feedback

"Winners can be self-reinforcing and require less praise. A manager can sometimes have a winner, but they're hard to find and cost money. The alternative is to hire a potential winner and train him."

—Blanchard and Johnson, *The One-Minute Manager*

An airline pilot once confided to me that on a flight from Los Angeles to Hawaii, his plane is off course ninety-eight percent of the time. Before I cancelled all my planned flights on his airline, he assured me that all planes experience the same problem. "Perfect direction is impossible," he said. "With movement comes error. 'George,' our name for the automatic navigation system, is constantly checking and making needed course corrections. If these frequent readings were not being taken, the plane could be halfway to Bora Bora before I realized it was off course. Without frequent monitoring and repositioning, the plane would eventually run out of fuel and splash down in the Pacific. Body surfing into the islands is not the way you want to arrive!"

As a leader, you help provide the instrument readings for your team. Without frequent feedback from you and the customer, the team can find it very difficult to maintain a true course. In our rapidly changing world, the target isn't a stationary one like Hawaii. As your team members' work requirements evolve, as new customer demands emerge, and as your strategic goals and priorities change, your organization's target is constantly in motion as well. You can't wait for a yearly review to make needed course corrections. Your feedback must keep your team focused on this ever-shifting island—or plunge your organization into the ocean.

Try a second example worth exploring. In the age of "smart missiles," traditional ballistic weapons are becoming obsolete. In modern warfare, it is no longer ready, aim, fire with stationary cannons launching shells on stationary targets. Now, it is ready, fire, aim!

Ready—at least point the weapon in the right direction!

Fire—get the missile airborne and in pursuit before they do it to you!

Aim—use your high-tech computer-driven tracking devices inside the projectile to home in on a moving aircraft that is trying to make evasive maneuvers!

Just like winners of modern wars, the victors in the corporate marketplace have the agility and the decisiveness to support quick action and flexible adjustment to day-to-day changes in the field.

The same is true of leaders trying to impact individual performance, a consistent, focused feedback can often be all that is needed to produce winning results. Uncertainty as to how one's work is being perceived from above can lead to unnecessary anxiety or, conversely, to a false sense of security. When a surprise is sprung in the form of a performance evaluation, a need for work to be redone, or an offhand remark, the employee can feel resentful and demotivated. When that happens you can start checking the Tokyo airport for your lost luggage.

We've devoted several chapters to the importance of balance, the balance between self-support and self-criticism, between support and accountability, between confrontational transactions and the need for bridge building. Feedback must be balanced as well. Prompt, non-judgmental negative feedback is a problem-solving instrument. It will keep your people on course with a minimum of tension and resentment. Appropriate positive feedback is a success-driving instrument. Recognition for work well done is rated by employees as second in importance only to monetary compensation as a performance motivator.

"Praise me or damn me, but don't just ignore me!"

—Rollo May

Unfortunately, too many managers allow their employees to wander off course or don't bother to define the destination. After it has become too late for minor course corrections, they heap on the bad news in a belligerent, confrontational manner that leaves the employee thinking about revenge. They hand out strokes for work well done with the same eagerness with which Scrooge McDuck gave away nickels. They wait until the going-away party or until the testimonial after the employee has died. In such situations feedback can't do much to promote productivity. Other managers use the pat-on-the-back merely as a buffer when handing out "constructive criticism." By that point, the criticism is rarely perceived as constructive or the strokes as sincere. How would you react if you found yourself in any of these situations?

> Howard Harlan chaired the language arts department at a large urban high school. When the district asked him to head a committee to draw up a new curriculum, he eagerly accepted, even though he knew it would mean long hours at no extra pay. Each week, he submitted a segment of the new curriculum to the district office. Though no response was immediately forthcoming, Howard interpreted the district's silence as an indication of their approval. Finally, after eleven weeks, Howard was called in to the district office. "I'm not exactly sure what we're looking for, but this isn't it," said the district supervisor. She handed him a folder full of papers representing hours of work on the part of Howard and his committee. "I think you'd better start from scratch and come up with something better." Howard stared at the folder, then threw it down on the desk. "I think you'd better come up with another chairperson," he said, stalking out of the office.

*　*　*　*　*　*

> Sunways Airlines seldom let the sun shine in on their employees. It was a bare-bones operation, and management considered compliments to be open invitations to complacency or demands for wage concessions. They even refused to show employees commendations from the flying public. Milford Meadows was a mechanic in good standing who often complained about management's lack of support. "Around here when they say nothing, consider it good news," he told the new employees. "The only reasons I stay are the benefits and the tight job market." Milford discovered that his work was appreciated only when he applied for a home loan. The loan officer required a letter from his boss. When the boss showed Milford the letter, Milford asked for a copy. As he put it, "That was the best news I ever received. I decided to add on to my house every year, just to find out how I was doing!"

*　*　*　*　*　*

> Tyrone Reese liked his job. He was a special-features writer for *Gourmand* magazine, and his editor, Celia Folder, thought his

work was "wonderful." That was fine. Except, to Celia, everybody's work was "wonderful." This made Tyrone just a little uneasy, but on the other hand what could be wrong with "wonderful"? Then one Friday afternoon, Celia came into his office. First she made a point of telling him how much everybody at *Gourmand* liked his work. Then she said, shyly, "I'm sorry to have to bring this up, I'm afraid you're not going to like this, but we have just a little problem here." The "little problem" was thirty pages of his copy that needed rewriting by Monday morning. "What can I do?" Celia said, sympathetically. "The publisher wants it redone. It's out of my hands. But you're such a fine writer, I know you'll handle it splendidly." As Tyrone watched his weekend plans fly out the window, he realized just how much Celia's "wonderfuls" really meant.

* * * * * *

Robin Lurie was an account manager at the L.A. office of Batterum, Barterum, Jung, Rubicon, and Associates; and Mother's Pies was her first big account. She was working sixty-five-hour weeks to develop and coordinate the fall media blitz, and everything she heard from the home office in New York was encouraging. Then, two weeks before the first magazine spreads were due for publication, the fertilizer hit the ventilator. The client was not pleased, and the agency was sending out their troubleshooter, Frank Ratsinato. A contact in the New York office warned Robin about Frank. "Watch out for him—he's a pit bull!" she was told. As luck would have it, an overturned truck on the freeway caused her to be ten minutes late that morning. She arrived in her office to find Frank waiting. "You flakes from L.A. are all the same!" were his first words to her. "Keeping banker's hours, it's no wonder you're behind." Frank found fault with Robin's scheduling, her choice of artists and copywriters, and the fact that her production manager ate his lunch at his drawing board. "We'll have to send a couple people out from New York to clean up this mess," he said as he left for the airport. Angry, dazed, and resentful, Robin wondered whether the home office had remembered to give "the pit bull" his distemper shots.

In each of these cases, the problem was feedback or the lack of it. Feedback was either too late in coming, unspecific, nonexistent, judgmental and abusive, openly insincere, or any combination thereof. In all cases, the results were destructive to the goals of manager and subordinate alike.

Care enough about yourself and your team to work at providing effective feedback. Follow these suggestions to provide feedback that will help the recipient stay on course.

Stay current with your feedback.

As we've discussed, immediacy in confronting a problem can be critical to your effectiveness. It can prevent a problem from ballooning into a crisis. The more immediate the information, the more useful it is. Give feedback when there is still time to do something about the problem. Don't wait until you are angry before you lay on the bad news, and don't wait for deadlines or evaluation time. If you do, you have only yourself to blame for your employees' resentment. No one likes being tried and convicted for something they didn't even know was against the law.

Timeliness applies to positive feedback as well. Immediate recognition has far more impact than delayed recognition. It is also experienced as more sincere. Initiate the contact yourself. The potency and perceived sincerity of your compliment will be that much greater than if the other party has to solicit it. Catch your people being effective.

Take time to share your support, even if it means making a special appointment to do so. Many managers use their return from lunch to scan each day for those who deserve recognition. They make a note in their to-do list to make sure they do it.

Some managers question the need for giving recognition beyond what is required at evaluation time. After all, isn't that taken care of twice a month by the person who brings around the paychecks? Sure, people will work for pay without verbal reassurance of their value, but how much more effectively will they work with such reassurance?

We all know this intuitively through our personal relationships, though few of us think of applying it to our professional relationships. When romantically involved, we often shower the one we love with statements of endearment and other "sweet nothings." This is known as the sales phase of any relationship. Once married, we too easily slip into the budget phase; we have to pay for all those dates! "I love you" gives way to "I love you, *too*," or "Can't you tell I love you?" As your spouse needs to be secure in your love, so your team members need to feel secure in your appreciation of their efforts. Frequent positive feedback will bring the point home. Once again, you will be providing a context that is conducive to your workers' self-motivation. This is not an obligation, but it is an opportunity to be taken advantage of.

Prepare a script that keeps your feedback specific and future-focused.

When you have negative feedback to deliver, take five minutes to prepare and rehearse your message. A prepared script can mean the difference between being heard and being resented.

Your script should have three components. A strong, opening "feeling" statement will get the other person's attention and give him a barometric reading of your concern: "I feel (uncomfortable, concerned, frustrated, irritated, downright angry), and I want to talk to you about it."

Then move quickly to your second statement, which defines the focus of the problem: "I'm concerned about. . . (some recent issue or behavior that has motivated the conversation), and I wanted to discuss it with you right away." Be specific about your concern. General criticisms invite defensiveness; specific ones lead naturally toward problem solving. Restrict your criticisms to specifics that you have observed, heard about (and confirmed!), or otherwise experienced. Specific feedback contributes to productive communication.

Be ready to inject some reassurance that suggests your expectation of positive change: "That's not like you; you're usually very responsible." Also be ready to state why the issue is important; people are more responsive to feedback when they understand why the problem matters. But before sharing either, take time to listen. Remember, all you have to go on is your own perception of the problem. You may not have all the facts, and the other person may already have found an acceptable way to handle the problem. She will always be more motivated to use her own solution than yours, and it may, in fact, be better than yours. Effective listening on your part may solve your problem while leaving her with the experience of having developed her own answer.

SCRIPTING YOUR FEEDBACK

I feel...

I'm concerned about...

In the future ...

If you listen, most such conversations will shift easily into the third, and most important, part of your script: identifying future expectations. The future must be the focus of any effective feedback. If you lose sight of this focus, you become a prosecuting attorney intent on getting a conviction rather than a manager interested in facilitating change. There's nothing that can be done about what's already happened. The problem is behind you; plan your script around the solution: "What can we do now to rectify the problem? What will we do next time to avoid the same problem?" Spend most of your time discussing these issues. They will keep you centered on the results you want and allow the other party to save face by contributing to the solution. Be ready to express your expectations by being able to complete your scripted message: "In the future, I would like you to. . . ," Your preparation will help you to specify the future performance you desire. Be as specific in your suggestions as you were in your criticism. Fuzzy expectations lead to fuzzy performance.

Even with effective feedback, not every confrontation will follow textbook models. Occasionally, you will run into someone who refuses to contribute to a solution, who won't even recognize that a problem exists, or who doesn't care to discuss it. With such responses, you feel like saying, "Don't you know you're supposed to follow my script?" Just

HERMAN

5/31

"I wanted a steady worker. You're absolutely motionless."

remember that it's change you want, not a conviction. Use comments that make her denial seem irrelevant: "This is not a trial. What's done is done. My concern is what we're going to do now and what we're going to do next time. In the future, I would like to see..."

If she continues with her denial: "Well, that's just the way I do things! And I'm not going to change", then try disengaging. Avoid forcing an agreement; you can't control her actions. Give her the distance to let her think about it without robbing her of dignity: "I understand that that is your choice, but I wanted to be clear about what I expected, and why. I would like you to think about it. " When you have clearly established what you want and have been assured that your message has been received and understood, end the conversation. You've given her the feedback; the next move is up to her. Resist any temptation to force your position. Pinching her jugular veins and shaking her into compliance may give you the illusion of victory, but be prepared to start searching for your luggage when the color returns to her face. People are more likely to hear your message and change their behavior when given time to reflect. Give them that time.

To avoid such frustrating discussions with difficult or defensive people, remember the value of giving them time to prepare their own reactions by setting up an appointment. This is a technique we introduced with regard to avoiding avoidance. Use the "I feel..." and "I'm concerned about..." parts of your script; then suggest a specific time to discuss future expectations. Often the hardest thing about receiving criticism is the element of surprise. A person's initial reaction may be denial and hostility, but later he may consider that you have a point. By giving him a warning, you allow him to go through the denial phase on his own. He may already have the problem solved by the time he walks into your office.

> *"A pat on the back is only a few vertebrae removed from a kick in the pants, but it is miles ahead in results."*
> —Ella Wheeler Wilcox

Keeping your feedback specific is a good idea when you're handing out the medals, too. General compliments convey no real information, and they can set the stage for complacency by putting workers on pedestals. (Remember Celia and her "wonderfuls"?) Recognition of specific achievements provides more useful information and is far more likely to be perceived as sincere. "I liked the way you planned the work schedule for the project" is far more effective than "Good job."

"I'd thank you Harrison, but, as you well know, yours is a thankless job."

Focus on good performances wherever and whenever you see them, and be creative in finding ways to show your appreciation. Give public acknowledgment of your workers' contributions. Take the time to tell others about the specific ways in which Charlie helped the organization. Put positive commendations in his personnel files; invite him to join you at meetings at which his projects will be discussed; talk positively about him behind his back. You're only as good as the people who work for you. Let others recognize and appreciate their accomplishments. Don't limit your recognition to your team members. Spread your recognition to your peers, your boss, even your customers—they all need it and deserve it.

Keep your positive feedback and your negative feedback separate from one another.

Far too many managers have been taught to use the "sandwich" or "pillow" technique when handing out bad news. They give the guy a goodie, zap him, and then dish out another goodie before ending the conversation: "Basically you're doing a fine job, but you blew it at that meeting yesterday. Don't worry, I'm sure you'll do fine." Using compliments to usher in criticisms and to cushion them diminishes the effectiveness of both messages. It dilutes the criticism, and it makes the compliments sound insincere. Yet it is so prevalent in today's business world that most of us have come to expect it. We seldom receive an on-the-job compliment without waiting for the other shoe to drop. We keep waiting for the "but": "Here it comes, here it comes. . . . There it is!"

Separate your messages whenever they can effectively stand alone. Performance evaluations by their nature are a summation of feedback given over a specific period of time. They are expected to include a combination of positive and negative feedback. But in your daily conduct of professional relationships, don't artificially force the good and bad news together. An uncompromised compliment is more effective in recognition of exceptional performance, and a confrontation that addresses a problem without a lot of leavening stresses the importance of resolving the problem.

There are times, of course, when you must deliver conflicting messages together. A school administrator would never tell a teacher, "I was concerned about your lack of disciplinary follow-through with Timmy. Why don't you come back this afternoon and I'll tell you what I liked about your class-control skills." If your messages must be mixed, lead with the criticism. Research indicates that most individuals, by far, prefer getting the bad news first. It gives them the opportunity to resolve the problem and end on a positive note. It allows them to savor the good news: "I'm concerned about the format you used for this illustration. I'd like to see a pie graph instead. I think it would better isolate the strength of our market share relative to the competition. I'm concerned about the format, but the focus of your analysis is right on target. Anyone reading this proposal will have a hard time discounting our strength."

Don't give feedback without first taking time to consider your follow through.

Any discussion of a serious problem is worth a follow-up conversation to assess progress. Arrange a follow-up appointment before you end the interview. Make a note of it in the other party's presence, and suggest that he do the same. Writing something in your calendar highlights the importance of what you have been talking about and assures you both of your commitment to solving the problem.

Most feedback sessions need never approach a discussion of consequences. But if an employee's performance has taken him below your eight thousand-foot level, specify the administrative action that will be taken if it continues to be deficient. You owe it to yourself, the employee, and your organization. Be clear as to what action will be taken if correction is not made: formal reprimand, suspension with probation, termination, or whatever the organization's established policy might be for such a situation.

In Chapter 4 we considered the problems of documentation and the route to termination in our discussion of accountability. If you handle negative feedback in a timely and procedural manner, you will avoid surprises both to the employee and, potentially, to the personnel and legal departments as well. Never make idle threats about firing or initiate documentation proceedings without a thorough knowledge of your organization's formal policies and procedures. As much as they hate sloppy or inadequate methodology, attorneys, personnel directors, and human resource specialists hate surprises. If you keep them informed and seek their advice when a problem first arises, they can be your allies. If you dump a full-blown crisis in their laps, don't be surprised if they act as though they are the employee's advocates instead of yours.

Use nonverbal communication for influence and reassurance.

The impression your words give to others can be augmented or neutralized by the way you are perceived . Rarely do we see ourselves as others see us. Few people will let you know how you are being perceived unless you ask them, or unless your habits border on the obnoxious.

> *"It is not sufficient to know what one ought to say, but one must also know how to say it."*
>
> —Aristotle

Take a minute to think about your notion of a manager who is effective at influencing others. Such managers command attention and project confidence not just by what they say, but by the way they communicate. As General Patton said, "A cold manner will never inspire confidence. A cold reserve cannot beget enthusiasm. There must be an outward and visible sign of inward and spiritual grace." Feedback will not be taken seriously if it is conveyed with a submissive countenance, downward-glancing eyes, and soft, hesitant speech patterns. Posture, eye contact, facial expression, physical positioning relative to the other person, hand gestures, and volume of speech all carry messages which are received as part of your feedback. They can convey like or dislike, affinity or indifference, self-confidence or insecurity, power or subordination. Learn how to use these tools of nonverbal communication to increase the effectiveness of your feedback. It may involve some conscious changes in habit and a little practice with a mirror and a tape recorder, but it will pay off in increased influence.

These changes start with an awareness of how you present yourself to others and with a motivation to make things happen. You can choose to adopt and practice new habits until they become part of you. Use the "Guidelines for Enhancing Nonverbal Communication" as a starting point for changing the way you present yourself.

Guidelines for Enhancing Nonverbal Communication

1 Show your regard for the other person by positioning yourself nearby, leaning toward him, nodding your head, and matching your words with your gestures and positioning. Avoid getting closer than two feet; few enjoy having their personal body space invaded.

2 Increase your persuasiveness through animation in your facial expressions, hand gestures, and speech intonation, rate, and volume. Use changes in your voice and facial expression to convey your feelings apart from the verbal content of your message. Such variations allow you to look serious when confronting and show warmth and a smile when supporting your staff.

3 Dress stylishly and neatly. "Dressing for success" won't impress everyone, but failing to do so will turn off many.

4 When listening, maintain constant eye contact, breaking it off only to make notes.

5 When speaking, maintain good eye contact while avoiding the constant stare. Break eye contact occasionally with an upward glance to avoid triggering the uncomfortable dominance game of who can stare the longest.

6 Use open-hand gestures that energize and bring color to your conversation.

7 Use touch professionally: shake hands, pat the person on the back, or touch a shoulder or forearm for emphasis. Avoid any contact that might be interpreted as sexual harassment with those who pull back from your touch.

8 Keep your voice strong enough to show emphasis and feeling through pitch variation.

Poorly handled feedback can precipitate destructive conflict. Well-handled feedback can short-circuit the need for conflict. Eliminating surprises can often make the difference. Keep your feedback timely, effective, and future-focused with every person you work with, and you will keep them all on an accurate course that will get you to your "Hawaii."

QUESTIONS WORTH ASKING

"I can prepare a script, but what do I do when the name-calling starts?"

Keep in mind that you will be called names only when others are not getting their way. Name-calling serves to divert the discussion to side issues that cannot be objectively decided, such as, "Am I fair or unfair?" "Do I have common sense, or have I lost it?" "Am I shortsighted or lopsided?" When someone calls you names, don't jump in with a counterattack. Listen to his input. If he offers a perspective that you have not considered, be flexible enough to change your mind. But be secure enough to hold firm on your decision if you feel it's the right decision. Deflect the anger with such statements as, "I understand what you're saying, and I understand your disappointment, but my answer remains the same." When you are confident in your ability to balance self-criticism with self-support, you are better prepared to change your mind if persuaded that you were in the wrong. The name-callers will then be better able to accept your decisions when you don't change your mind. They will do you one better than liking you—they will respect you.

"Is there such a thing as giving too much recognition?"

Yes, but most managers err on the side of not giving enough. Use the sincerity test. Do you mean it? If the answer is "yes," share your recognition. If the answer is "no," then don't. Don't place your workers on pedestals. For recognition to be perceived as sincere, it must be earned, and it must be given out relatively infrequently. When it's handled right, positive feedback is sincere, specific, and self-initiated. It's hard for any leader to give out too much of that kind of recognition.

KEEPERS

☐ Use feedback for course corrections in a changing world.

☐ Keep criticism specific and future-focused.

☐ Catch people being effective.

☐ Keep positive feedback self-initiated, specific, separate, and sincere.

☐ Listen before suggesting solutions.

☐ Think change, not conviction.

☐ Performance evaluations should not be a surprise but a reflection of ongoing feedback.

CHAPTER EIGHT

Keeping Your Big Mouth Shut: Cultivating the Listening Edge

"As you go through life you are going to have many opportunities to keep your mouth shut. Take advantage of all of them."

—James Dent

If as managers we fail to receive and understand what our subordinates are trying to communicate, we miss out on information that may be useful to us in making decisions. We waste time and money on ill conceived endeavors that might never get off the drawing board if we encouraged and listened to valid criticism. And we lose respect and cooperation. If we are perceived as not listening, we fuel resistance and resentment. We are less likely to be listened to. People become less willing to act on our advice if they feel they are being shut out.

It's one thing to confront others; it is an entirely different matter to be confronted yourself. How do you, as a manager, respond to kibitzing or criticism from your workers? And how do you think they would gauge your response? One of the most respected Fortune 500 companies recently surveyed its employees on the issue of managerial responsiveness. The employees were asked what they thought would be the result of their sharing with their boss "a better way of doing their work." Their responses broke down into three roughly equal groups. One-third of the workers thought that their boss would listen, a change would occur, and they would be rewarded in some way for their innovation. Another third thought that their boss would listen but that no real change would occur. And one-third felt that they would be punished in some way for expressing an idea counter to their boss's.

Whether those workers' expectations would actually have occurred, we cannot know. But the fact that two-thirds of the workers felt that their bosses would not listen is cause for concern. Communication is a two-way process. If what is being transmitted isn't being received, it's not communication. Want more proof? In another study, managers were rated by their co-workers in terms of "general effectiveness in understanding and being understood by others through reading, writing, speaking, and listening." When the high- and low-rated managers were compared, the only significant difference between the two groups turned out to be in their definitions of communication. The low-rated group talked about communication as a one-way process of sending, while the high-rated group included the receiving and understanding of information in their definitions.

By permission of Johnny Hart and Creators Syndicate, Inc.

One reason we fail to listen to criticism or suggestions is that many of us are simply not very good at listening. We were given formal training in reading, writing, and (in many instances) public speaking, but none or very little in effective listening. "Unlike hearing," Thomas Anastasi, Jr. has written, "listening demands total concentration. Listening is an active search for meaning, while hearing is passive."

When we listen passively, we allow ourselves to be distracted. Our environment is saturated with distractions; piles of paper, the media, pressing deadlines, a never-ending stream of interruptions and phone calls. One manager described life in his office as "information overload; it was like trying to sip through a straw from a fire hydrant." With those kind of distractions, it is easy to understand why we fail to listen well. If we don't like what someone is saying, we can just tune in to a different channel. Too many times we have an *open door*, but a *closed mind*. We allow our assumptions of what the speaker is going to say block out what he is really saying. We interpret the speaker's words substituting our own databank of probable statements. Unfortunately, what we think we are hearing isn't what is being said at all. If you're too busy to work at listening, you're too busy. You've all had managers who failed to listen; you know how it made you feel.

"Listening does not mean simply maintaining a polite silence while you are rehearsing in your mind the speech you are going to make the next time you can grab a conversational opening. Nor does listening mean waiting alertly for flaws in the other fellow's arguments so that later you can mow him down."

—S. I. Hayakawa

A second reason we fail to listen has nothing to do with laziness, distractions, or lack of skills. Too often we are striving for an appearance of unity and harmony at the expense of openness and dialogue. We call meetings to "discuss" possible changes; we encourage "brainstorming" among our staff. But then we subtly silence the critics and support only those who rubber-stamp our ideas. We cultivate the image of being listeners, but in fact we shut out most ideas that are not in harmony with our own.

We do this because we equate consensus with total agreement, and view resistance as a problem that must be silenced or overcome. Resistance that has surfaced is one of the greatest gifts a manager can be given. Poorly handled conflict causes problems; conflict that is managed well can create opportunities. Conflict can be an asset that allows a variety of ideas and perspectives to be voiced, considered, and processed. It can lead to a wider understanding of a problem and a greater choice of alternatives for its solution. It can enable us to cut our losses before ideas are fixed in cement. It can allow us to learn from our mistakes and prevent us from making public fools of ourselves. It can stimulate healthy interaction and a feeling of involvement and cohesion among our workers. A dialogue that makes room for conflict allows you and your staff to deal with your concerns openly and reach a consensus. There need not be unanimity on decisions and policies.

"Our culture definitely rewards independent thought, and we often have constructive disagreements—at all levels. It doesn't take a new person long to see that people feel fine about openly disagreeing with me. That doesn't mean I can't disagree with them, but it does mean that the best ideas win. . . . Don't get hung up on who owns the idea. Pick the best one, and let's go."

—Steve Jobs, NeXT and Apple founder

Even if a particular team member's idea does not carry the day, there can be an easing of resistance if dissenters feel that their positions have been listened to, understood, and considered before the decisions are made and the policies set. Without such a consensus, you may be faced with the other kind of conflict—the kind that gets your bags sent to Japan:

> George Grippe was the bright new MBA at Bonzo Productions, but it didn't take an MBA to see that his crew's production figures were down. He had been hired to bring in new ideas, and he had done that, but they just didn't seem to be working. Staring at the wall of the bathroom stall, George found nothing there to enlighten him. His contemplation was broken by the conversation of two of his workers as they entered the room: "He's piling it deeper and wider," one of them said. "He's got all these great ideas, but he hasn't spent two minutes with us since he got here. He wants it all his way; I say let him have it. The damn hot shot! At the rate he's pushing the equipment, it'll burn out in a week. Then we'll see how far his MBA gets him."

*　*　*　*　*　*

Hector Mushmouth was President, CEO, and generalissimo at Waterloo Electronics. He had created the Waterloo 280 computer and had watched it soar out of his garage to the top of the high-tech hit parade. But for the last six quarters, he had been watching his "baby" die a slow death. It was being throttled by Korean competition. He had tried to force old solutions into a new package, but the public wasn't buying, and neither were his engineers or his marketing staff. The only ideas that ever got aired were Hector's, and his crew (those who hadn't already abandoned the sinking ship) were tired of his lies and rationalizations. At the quarterly management meeting, Hector's voice echoed through the conference room, bouncing off the blank, staring faces with little or no effect. "I know that this quarter's numbers aren't what they should be," he proclaimed, "but there is light at the end of the tunnel. If we pull together, our new line will..." They had all heard this sugar-coated whitewash before. Everyone knew that the only way they'd ever find any light was by getting out of the tunnel altogether. The boss was unwilling or unable to find the way.

*　*　*　*　*　*

The new "open-door" policy was in place at Synergy Systems. Employees had been encouraged to speak up and make suggestions. But Debra Lance was so busy getting things done that she never stopped to evaluate why so few of her employees were taking advantage of her "openness." The words were all there, but Debra's actions did nothing to support the new policy. The door was open, but as far as Debra's employees could see, her mind was closed. When anyone did stop by to share his concerns or offer suggestions, Debra would continue with her work, offering him no more than ten percent of her attention. Suggestions were submitted but never acknowledged; nothing was ever changed. After a while, people stopped trying.

"You have not converted a man because you have silenced him."

—John Morley

When we fail to listen, when we silence resistance and criticism, we sow dragon seeds. Left alone to flourish they can grow into healthy, full-grown dragons that can sap the energy, morale, and productivity of your organization. In Chapter 5, we discussed the problem of avoidance. It is important to recognize that when your people feel that their input is being ignored, it can lead to an avoidance situation in reverse, that is, one in which their frustration levels build up over a reluctance to confront you. Your staff members are as uncomfortable about conflict as you were before you started reading this book. Probably more so. For all they know, pursuing a confrontation with their manager could cost them their jobs. We know from our own experience what happens when someone avoids confronting a problem—it turns into a bigger problem! Some staff will just leave a poison pen letter for an exit interview. Others will let it surface in an aggressive outburst. Their anger gives

Reprinted by permission of Newspaper Enterprise Association, Inc.

them a "reason" (and the courage) to confront you. Under such circumstances their criticism will be unspecific and highly emotional: "I'm the only one around here who knows what she's talking about!" "Why the hell should I listen to you; you never listen to me!"

It's one thing to understand; it's quite another to know how to defuse the emotions before dealing with the issues in a manner conducive to problem solving. Unfortunately such situations may catch us off guard. Our typical response is one of flight or fight, guilt-peddling or threat. Either we back off, often denying that a problem exists ("Who me? What did I do?"), or we counterattack ("Oh, yeah? You're not so hot either, Jack, and I'll tell you why!"). Of course both responses escalate resistance. The confrontation degenerates further into shouting and name-calling. By then neither one of you is listening. Effective listening can be used to handle even the most difficult attack. There are three steps to disarm and use resistance that parallel our script for appropriate criticism:

LISTENING TO DISARM ANGER

1   Absorb and accept the feelings.
2   Explore and understand the problem.
3   Redirect to problem solving.

It's up to you to avoid the defensive or aggressive response. Start by learning to manage your own self-confidence as we discussed in Chapter 3. Your self-worth should not be on the line every time you make an error. If you keep your self-feedback balanced, the thought that you might have made a mistake should not trigger the flight-or-fight alarm. Each mistake gives you the opportunity to learn something no matter who points it out. You're not on trial. You simply have a problem that needs to be solved.

> *"I am never defeated. . . . It is not because my technique is faster than that of the enemy. . . . The fight is finished before it has begun. . . . [Aikido] is not a technique to fight with or to defeat the enemy. It is a way to reconcile the world and to make human beings one family."*
>
> —O-Sensei, founder of aikido

Absorb and accept the feelings expressed.

In dealing with resistance, a manager might do well to consider the Japanese martial art aikido. No, we're not suggesting that you handle resistance in Chuck Norris fashion. The aikido practitioner seeks to counter an attack without bringing harm to the attacker. The idea is to preserve balance; to restore harmony to the relationship. If your organization often seems driven by conflict, you might want to bring some of that harmony into your office.

As a manager, you can restore harmony in the face of conflict without harming the person attacking you. Instead of silencing the other party, listen, absorb, and redirect his attack. Instead of meeting force with force, use the attack to explore the problem. To his, "You don't know what you're talking about!" you might respond, "Sometimes that's true. Have you been talking to my husband? He feels the same way about me. Where do you see a problem?" In honoring his resistance you give him validation without accepting the severity of his attack. At best, you will receive information that will be valuable in solving the problem. At the very least, you will gain useful knowledge; you will almost certainly come away with a better understanding of his position. "I'm glad you pointed this out to me," you can tell him. "I wasn't aware we had such a problem. I think I'd feel the same way in your situation." Do not reiterate your position at this point; do not try to get him to see things your way. Just letting him know you're willing to listen will help disarm his anger. You can talk about your position later. Do not reinforce his resistance, but acknowledge it. Let him know it's okay to disagree, but unless he has truly convinced you that you're wrong, do not commit yourself to supporting his position.

TECHNIQUES OF VERBAL AIKIDO

Try some of these statements in response to verbal attacks:

ATTACK	AIKIDO RESPONSE
"It won't work."	"It may not. I see some problems. What do you see?"
"You're just like the rest of the managers around here!"	"I am a manager, but I also want to hear what you're saying. What do you see as the problem?"
"All you think about is your department!"	"I am concerned about what happens to my department, as you are about yours. But I'm also concerned about working together. What's the problem?
"You women are all the same!"	"I'm glad you noticed. But whatever you think about women, I want to work with you, not against you. What is the problem?"
"You aren't fair!"	"I'm sure sometimes I'm not. Help me understand how you see it."
Any attack	"There may be some truth to that. I don't have any illusions of being perfect. What's the problem as you see it?"

Such verbal aikido is of course easier to read about than to practice. All too often our response to the unexpected confrontation is good old Western kicking, biting, and gouging. By the time we gain control of ourselves, it is often too late. In such situations, learn to be aware of your impending loss of control and to distance yourself responsibly: "Before you or I say something we are going to regret, why don't we both take an hour to think about the problem. Let's get back together and talk then." After you've given yourselves an hour to cool off, you will both be ready for a more constructive dialogue about the problem.

Sometimes even a five-minute break can be useful: "Please have a seat," you might say. "I need to get the project file. It will just take a minute." Even the brief time it takes you to leave your desk and shut the door may be all you need to gather your thoughts before responding. You can now prepare to listen instead of reacting.

Once you've made the decision to listen and have absorbed the initial attack, help the other party calm down. Keep your voice low, without taking on a patronizing tone. Use calming hand gestures. Keep your palm open and move it slowly in an up and down motion. Smile and make frequent eye contact. If the other person is not sitting down, invite her to do so. You might say something like, "Now that you've got my attention, I want to hear what you have to say. Let's both sit down and talk about it."

Explore and understand the problem.

You have acknowledged the problem and expressed your concern. Now it's time to explore the problem. To convince her that you're really listening, grab a pencil and paper to take notes. Note taking is an aid to active listening and to keeping your concentration focused. You can't be jumping ahead to what you're going to say if you're writing down accurately what the other person is saying. It signifies to her that you are taking her seriously. It also brings accountability into the conversation. She will be more likely to keep her side of the discussion substantive and less likely to descend to the level of name-calling. It will also give you something to do other than to glare at her across your desk. If she objects she can usually be mollified with an explanation: "I take notes so that I can remember. I want to make sure that we take care of the problem. If you would like a copy I would be glad to give you one."

At the heart of this approach is the concept of active listening. When you apply this technique, it assures the other party that you understand what she is trying to communicate. Practice the following techniques of active listening:

Listen with respect.

Avoid jumping to conclusions and applying labels. Don't focus on key words or phrases that may lead you to pigeonhole the other party and to ignore what he is really trying to convey. Don't allow the person's position, politics, age, or status to lead you to think that you know what he's going to say before he says it. Listen closely: he may be telling you something entirely different.

> *"The only man I know who behaves sensibly is my tailor; he takes my measures anew each time he sees me. The rest go on with their old measurements and expect me to fit them."*
> —George Bernard Shaw

Likewise, don't allow previous run-ins with the person to prejudice you against his current input. Don't switch him off just because the last idea he came up with was a turkey or because he dresses funny or talks too loud in the break room. Pay attention to now, to the current situation and the current set of circumstances.

Listen to understand, not to gain tactical advantage.

People in this situation will seldom settle for what you want unless part of your concern is with finding something that they want. If you're striving to win at the other person's expense, you may win the battle and lose the war. Winners never always win because losers never forget. People who are not necessarily articulate are, nevertheless, able to find creative ways of sending your bags to Japan. Active listening promotes win/win interaction in which both of you come away with some of your needs met. Take the trouble to try to understand the other party's needs. Make every effort to put yourself in her position, and try to comprehend the situation from her perspective.

Many sales programs use this concept to develop a consultative selling model; one in which salespeople learn to assist the buyer. They resist pushing through a sale that is not needed; doing so may cost them a customer. Whenever you attempt to influence others you are a salesperson. Sell yourself as an active, respectful listener.

Know what the speaker really means.

Avoid "common sense" assumptions that can lead to misunderstandings. When people are emotional, they tend to attack with general, ambiguous statements. Asking questions is the most obvious way to clarify what has been said. Help her to be specific by asking, "What happened?" or "What specifically did I (he, she) do?" When she has finished making her point you may want to paraphrase what she has said to be sure you have understood it as she intended it: "Let me see if I understand. You feel frustrated because I . . ." Be specific. Make sure you understand the issue under discussion. Paraphrasing forces the angry party to listen. The resulting interruption of her tirade helps to reduce her anger. Even if your interpretation is not quite right, she will appreciate your attempt to understand how she feels as well as what she has said. And with such encouragement, she will be certain to explain herself more clearly.

One of the biggest obstacles to effective listening is the assumption that the same words mean the same thing to all people. The meaning of a word lies in its user, not in the word itself. Our own associations are necessary for helping us think; unfortunately they can also be the source of misunderstanding. Good listeners seek active clarification. They are not afraid to say, "I'm not sure what you mean. Will you clarify that for me?" By asking specifically, "What is your objection?" and "What would you prefer?" you force him to answer specifically. Either he will give you a clear statement of his view of the problem, or he will back off.

Listen with questions in mind.

You can facilitate this skill by taking notes. Jot down your questions as you're jotting down his ideas; then ask for clarification later. Some of the questions you might ask yourself are: "What is he saying? Does it follow what he said previously? What's his point? Is it making any sense? Do any pieces seem to be missing? Are his points backed up with evidence? Is this fact, opinion, assumption, or complete hogwash? What are his sources for this information? Am I allowing my prejudices to color what he's trying to tell me? Is my ego getting in the way? How does what he's telling me relate to what I already know? How useful is his information? How might I apply it?" Listening with such questions in mind can keep you from becoming distracted and prematurely tuning out.

Be a good facilitator.

Take responsibility for the success of the discussion. Being an active listener means more than just having good ears and perceptive eyes. You're not watching television here. Keep the other person comfortable by showing an active interest in what she's saying. "Closed" questions that can be answered in one word can shut down a conversation. Use "open" questions that encourage more than one-word responses: "How? In what way?"; "What problems do you see if . . .?" An animated expression, a nod of the head, even a Mr. Spock eyebrow raise can encourage him to keep talking. Try an occasional word of encouragement such as "I can understand that"; "That's interesting"; "You're kidding!"; "Tell me more." Such comments bring you, the listener, to life and keep the other party in the "talking seat." On the other hand, avoid distracting interruptions. Nothing will so readily convince the other party that you're not really sincere about your interest.

> *"Bore: a person who talks when you want him to listen."*
> —**Ambrose Bierce**, *The Devil's Dictionary*

Don't be afraid of silence. Many managers are so uncomfortable with silence that they use a pause in the conversation to fill the room with their own voice. Use a pause in a positive way to suggest that you want the other person to continue talking. But remember also that too much active listening can create discomfort. Remember that our purpose in listening is to understand the problem as she sees it. After disarming her anger, you need to be forthcoming about how you hope to deal with the problem.

Redirect to problem solving.

Once you have used active listening to explore the problem, it's time to move on to resolution. As with other aspects of conflict that we've talked about in this book, the emphasis must be on present and future problem solving, not on past difficulties and animosities. Soon it will be your turn to respond; be ready to give an honest, direct response. At worst, he may still be disappointed; but through your effective listening, he will know that he has been heard and understood. Often that is all that is necessary to bring about a workable compromise.

Explore any suggestions the other party may have for resolving the problem.

Just as when we gave negative feedback, listening is preferable to telling. Start by asking future-focused questions that move the conversation toward problem solving: "What do you want to do now?" "How do you want this to be handled next time?" "How do you suggest we resolve this problem?" Listen actively, and don't share your suggestions until you have explored hers. If her input is acceptable to you, the conversation is as good as over. If not, now it's your turn to suggest an acceptable compromise. You have listened to her; now it's her turn to listen to you. Chances are she will. Listening makes listeners.

Be ready to state your own feelings, needs, and views.

Be brief, sincere, and non-provocative. Define the problem in terms of needs, not just solutions. Explain any aspects of the situation that are not open to compromise, such as government restrictions, safety regulations, or policy that has been decided upon higher up in the organization. If you have been convinced by some of her arguments, now is the time to let her know. But be firm about stating your reasons why other aspects of your position must remain unchanged. Make it clear that you are searching for a middle ground, a position that is acceptable to both of you.

Check where you both now stand on the issue.

Once you have stated your position, find out whether the other party has altered his. What does he like about your policy or proposal now?

How could it benefit his working situation? Avoid asking "why" questions that can force him back into a position of defensiveness. Instead, ask "what" and "how" questions that focus on the future. He may, like Melville's Bartleby, simply balk at what you want him to do: "I would prefer not to." Ask him, "What would you suggest as an alternative?" not "Why are you acting this way?" Keep on brainstorming possible solutions. Work toward a solution that will meet both of your needs without generating new problems, and develop a plan for its implementation.

Deflect any non-substantive resistance that remains.

At this point, you will have dealt with the substantive issues between you. If you encounter further resistance, or if the compromise position remains unacceptable, you may have to deflect the residual dissatisfaction or simply end the conversation. You do not need to seek closure every time; sometimes a win/win agreement is not possible. That is why lines of authority are established. When both sides have been heard, someone has to make a decision. But if the other party has been listened to, some comments can be dealt with without upsetting the balance and spirit of cooperation you have achieved. Try some of the following parries, but do not let yourself be put on the defensive.

RESISTANCE: "I've got too much to do as it is. Why don't you give this job to Marian?"

REFOCUS: "I know you've been working hard, but I think that you're best suited to this project. We can put some of your other projects on hold."

RESISTANCE: "I'll schedule some time for it the week after next."

REFOCUS: "What pressing projects do you have that would prevent you from starting on it tomorrow? I'd rather put those on hold. "

RESISTANCE: "The other guys won't like this either."

REFOCUS: "You may be right; I'll check it out with them. But right now, my major concern is that we both understand what is expected."

RESISTANCE: "You owe me one!"

REFOCUS: "Yes, and I haven't forgotten. But this is one I can't give in on. I need your help. I'll have to carry that debt a little longer."

RESISTANCE: "But we've always done it the other way."

REFOCUS: "And it's always worked, I know. However, this is a new problem, and it calls for a different approach."

RESISTANCE: "Well, I still can't see it your way."

REFOCUS: "I understand that, and I might feel the same way if I were you. But the fact remains that I'm willing to go only this far, and I expect you to follow through."

Even if the other person goes away disappointed, he will know he has been listened to. Never be afraid of disappointing people. If their disappointment comes from an environment of support and mutual respect, they will recover quickly. Employee dissent should not be taken as a sign of disharmony; it can be a sign of their trust in your ability and willingness to listen. It is when dialogue stops that you should be concerned.

Whatever the outcome, invite him to approach you earlier next time if a similar problem comes up. Make it clear that you prefer a current assertive message. Where possible, set a follow-up date to check back with him to be sure the problem is being taken care of. You can use this session to take care of any residual difficulties. Effective follow-up will help you avoid a future escalation of conflict. Again you are building a history of being a problem solver, not a problem evader.

> *"Our sudden fascination with Japanese management and quality circles is, to a great extent, simply no more than the development of and commitment to a comprehensive listening program. A wise man once said, 'When two people say you are drunk, lie down.' Likewise, when two employees say there is a better way, listen! . . . Our obsession with action ignores the importance of listening first."*
> —**Michael H. Mescon and Timothy Mescon**

By listening effectively in a conflict situation, you put to rest the notion that your working relationships always have to be harmonious. Let differences be aired and discussed; model appropriate ways of handling disagreements. Encourage directness within your working group. Dealing with conflict directly may be uncomfortable, but if handled well it can lead to positive change and mutual respect. It can help to discharge the disappointment and resentment that almost inevitably snowball into serious problems when conflict is suppressed. Factions form, productivity suffers, and valued people leave. Timing, tact, and distancing yourself to think about your message will always have their place; but never underestimate the power of open dialogue.

"The role is marked by involvement more than by telling . . .
We say to chief executive officers: Paint the picture, paint the
vision, preach the story. At the same time, remember that
listening and involvement are the ways that you'll pull it off."

—Tom Peters

Listening is more than a conflict management tool; it's the heart and soul of effective leadership. Allow yourself time for listening. Don't give people the impression that you're too busy to listen. By making yourself accessible and inviting problems to surface, you ensure that major, aggressive confrontations are far less likely to occur.

Effective leaders don't wait for problems to come to them; they build in regular time to let problems surface. In Chapter 6 we mentioned Peters and Waterman's concept of MBWA—Management By Wandering Around. MBWA is not just for bridge building. It also makes you accessible for the discussion of problems among your staff. If that's not adequate, use the start of your one-on-ones to prompt for any problems.

Lee Iaccoca suggested starting private reports with what he called "red flags": any potential problems that could grow into big problems. By regularly scheduling time to clear the air, conflicts never had a chance to fester out of control.

"Try to imagine how much I care!"

If you take the time to listen, care enough to work at listening well. Don't continue working while trying to listen. In other words, never pretend to listen. Unless the other person is completely insensitive, she will notice the glazed-over eyes and pasted-on smile. Give her your full attention. Keep your eyes focused on the speaker, and your attention will remain there. By sharpening your sensitivity to feelings, you can improve your timing.

One manager, calling for cost estimates from her design department, heard the tension in the voice of her counterpart when he answered. Instead of asking for information, she acknowledged the feeling by saying, "Don't tell me. Let me guess. I bet I'm the twentieth interruption you've had this morning!" After a short laugh and five minutes of listening, she got full cooperation and a well-deserved "Thanks for calling."

> *"There go my people. I must find out where they are going so I can lead them."*
>
> —Alexandre Ledru-Rollins

Being an effective listener is a challenge. And yet we know that the perceptive listener has the edge. The results of listening can be dramatic; a satisfied customer who will come back, a negotiated settlement that leaves both sides pleased, an understanding by a parent of a child's needs, and a team of workers who trust and respect their manager. Make the effort to be a manager who works at listening. It is more than a skill; it is an attitude of openness that expresses, "I have something to learn from every person I meet." What an opportunity!

QUESTIONS WORTH ASKING

"It's true. I'm easily distracted when I'm trying to listen. How can I get out of the noise?"

Learn from the media. When they want your attention, they use color, volume, rapid animation, and other grabbers. You don't have to train your people to jump up and down, but you can suggest that they use a preamble to get your attention before proceeding. Have them try such attention-getting openers as, "I've got something important I want to discuss with you." Don't listen to everything; work at listening to what matters.

"I don't seem to be able to stop tuning people out. Isn't there anything I can do about it?"

As one manager put it, "listen louder." Work at keeping your concentration focused, allowing people to complete their thoughts. If you must associate to other thoughts, avoid going off on tangents by staying in the vicinity of the speaker's concept, that is, associating to thoughts and experiences that relate to the subject of the conversation. Finally, learn to verify the accuracy of your reception by restating the central message. Advise others about how to keep your attention with statements such as, "I've got something different I want to discuss with you." The cue "different" can alert you to listen.

"I know I'm supposed to keep an open door, but I can't do it all the time. How do I avoid turning off my employees?"

Let your people know when you are most approachable and how they can get your attention appropriately when you're not. One manager used an antique traffic light in front of his office. Red meant, "Unless blood is involved, don't interrupt, or it may be yours." Yellow meant, "Caution; use your judgment." Green meant, "I'm open; it's a good time to talk." He was on green forty-five percent of the day, and people appreciated it. They never had to guess when it was the right time to approach him. Help your own people to avoid guesswork and catch you when you're most receptive. Use your door; if it's open, you're open. If it's closed, they will know to hold off unless it's important.

"It's one thing to disarm an angry person, but how do I deal effectively with a whole group of angry people?"

It's more difficult, but you can apply the same tools. It's just more imperative that you do it well. Groups will say things that individuals usually won't. It's called the "wolf-pack phenomenon." Use your active-listening skills, but move your focus from "the pack" to individuals by saying, "I want to hear what you're saying, but I'm having a hard time handling all your comments at once. Margaret, you seem to have some strong feelings about this. What are your main concerns?" As you listen actively to Margaret, write down her points on a flip chart, overhead projector, or simple notepad. As an individual, Margaret will tend to be more focused and responsible than as a member of a "pack." Move around the group to learn the concerns of other people. Then use the energy of the conflict to move the group toward problem solving: "I understand your concerns. What are you suggesting we do?" Write down their ideas, but do not make a decision on the basis of a single emotional meeting. Give everyone time to think. Tell them, "This is too important a decision to make a snap judgment about it. I'll have these notes typed up and copied for all of you. Let's think about it and meet again in two weeks. Thanks for speaking up on this; it's obviously a problem we need to deal with."

"You keep mentioning one-on-one's. How should a manager structure them, and how frequently should they occur?"

In our rapidly changing world, many managers find value in scheduling one-on-one's weekly with every subordinate and their boss. If you limit sessions to twenty minutes, both parties will learn to stick to important agenda items and use the time wisely. Instead of feeling a pressure to talk, managers can make better use of the time by asking regular questions that structure the time. What you ask for is what they will learn to give you:

- "What are the 'red flags' we have to deal with this week?"

- "What's working for you? What have you done particularly well this week?"

- "What are your major goals (priorities) for this week?"

- "What do you need from me to do your job?"

- "What are you doing differently?"

Optional questions worth asking at intervals:

- "What training do you feel you need to meet your goals three years from now?"

- "What have you been reading or hearing that we ought to be aware of as a department?"

- "Are you still getting what you want in this position? What career goals do you have that I can help you reach?"

- "Have you had any funny incidents happen this week?"

Regular meetings instill accountability while providing a supportive context for educational and motivational follow-up. Problems get noticed and handled immediately instead of waiting for distant deadlines to surface. There can be no favorites for managers; one-on-ones guarantee regular, equal access for all subordinates.

"My first message is: Listen, listen, listen to the people who do the work."

—H. Ross Perot

KEEPERS

☐ Don't silence resistance, use it to make better decisions.

☐ Listen to, understand, and assist others; promote win/win problem solving.

☐ Avoid mindreading; listen to what people are saying, not to what you expect them to say.

☐ In problem solving, use your ears and eyes more than your mouth.

☐ Absorb, explore, and redirect any verbal attack.

☐ To disarm anger, acknowledge the problem and your desire to listen.

☐ Use active listening, ask for specifics, take notes, and move on to future-focused problem solving.

☐ Check important messages: repeat what was said to assure that it has been received.

☐ Be a good facilitator: use open questions, paraphrases, animation, door openers, and the positive pause.

☐ Encourage others to come to you early with disagreements or problems.

CHAPTER NINE

Conflict Up the Organization: Managing Your Boss

"If you want to succeed, do everything possible to help your boss do his or her job."

—Abram Collier

As you've been reading this book, you've probably been making mental notes about applying specific strategies to people you work with. Very likely you've noticed that there's one area we haven't addressed: How do you manage conflict when the direction is up the organization? You're a manager, but unless you're the CEO, you have to answer to a boss.

Good leaders know that a positive working relationship with the boss involves a sensitive balance mixing support with conflict. That balance can limit their effectiveness if it's not handled well. They also recognize that the burden for managing the relationship cannot, and should not, rest entirely with the boss. No boss is perfect; their people skills and wisdom are not necessarily greater than those of their team members. No boss has unlimited time, encyclopedic knowledge, or extrasensory perception. Effective leaders do not wait for their boss to manage them well; they take the initiative of managing their boss in order to maximize results for themselves, their boss, and their organization.

However, the very nature of lines of authority can set the stage for frustration when the boss blocks or constrains our actions. Sometimes we find ourselves at odds with even the best bosses; sometimes for good reasons. Problem solving must move in both directions along the lines of authority. The same could be said about handling peers. Team members and managers must have the fortitude and the skills to confront up and across the organization. The cost of avoidance can be great. At the very least, it can mean resistance, low productivity, and erosion of morale. At worst, it can lead to disaster and a potential organizational liability.

> *"Don't be afraid to be firm with authority, even if it means a little respectful shouting."*
>
> —Stanley Bing

We must have truth up the organization, but confronting a boss without support and cooperation can be like striking a match near a leaking gas tank. It cannot be done without a healthy insurance policy—a history of bridge building, trust and respect that gives you the confidence to confront your boss without losing your reputation as a team player. All bosses like to be right, but most are capable of admitting errors and of learning from them. Mature bosses are more concerned with results than with being right. They can move beyond their jealousy and defensiveness if they are brought to realize that such attitudes are incompatible with the goals of the organization. The vast majority of bosses can handle direct, early problem solving, and many may even encourage it. As one boss put it to his new hire, "Don't confuse authority with wisdom. Just because I have authority doesn't mean I'm right. I expect you to confront me when I need it. That's part of your job here."

> *"There is one point on which I have some real concern. It has to do with the cautious attitude of so many young men in middle management today. They seem reluctant to stick their necks out or to bet on a hunch.*
>
> *"This is not always because they lack nerve. Sometimes they make the mistake of thinking that top management places a greater premium on following form than on anything else. I wish we could stir them up a bit and encourage a little more recklessness among this group of decision makers. Every time we've moved ahead in IBM, it was because someone was willing to take a chance, put his head on the block, and try something new."*
>
> —Thomas J. Watson, Jr.

With most people, scripting a confrontation with your organizational peers or superiors is not much different from what we learned in Chapter 7 about giving feedback to employees. One still needs to be specific and future-focused. There is one glaring difference. As you may suspect, documentation does not work with bosses and is not much more effective with peers. If you say to your boss, "If you keep acting this way, I'm going to document you," she's not likely to take it as "just kidding." It's like threatening to document your spouse: "After three instances of failing to put the cap back on the toothpaste, I'm going to send a note to your mother." Such statements are rarely well received or even considered.

It is seldom wise to initiate a crusade against any peer or manager. Instead, sell her on a cost/benefit analysis. Do some homework to find support for your position, then suggest to her how the organization would benefit from following your course of action. Never push too hard for your position; doing your homework and giving the boss time to think are almost always more effective.

It's not hard to tell when your feedback is threatening your boss. His eyeballs get large, his voice rises, he leans forward in his chair. Take the hint. You may have gone too far. Use diplomacy to defuse what he perceives as a threat: "I understand it's your decision, and whatever you decide, I'll do what I can to make it work. But I would appreciate it if you'd think about this alternative." Such statements keep your assertiveness in perspective. You are offering feedback, not an attack on your boss's authority or ego.

With a peer, try to come to an understanding of her position and her decision to make priority judgments that are different from yours. (Who knows? Her boss may have told her that her project is more important than yours.) Instead of cajoling, try to get her to understand your position: "I know you have to make your own decisions on what your priorities are, but I need for you to understand that unless I get your input by next Tuesday, I can't meet my deadline." If no agreement seems reachable, if egos, power games, the mania for winning, or just plain differences in priority seem to be running counter to your interests, it may be wise to seek an authoritative judgment. But even so, keep the conflict eyeball to eyeball. Instead of "going over her head," suggest that the two of you go together to the boss for a clarification.

Unfortunately, not all managers are fortunate enough to work for responsive peers and bosses. Managing even difficult peers is usually viable, but how does one deal with ego-obsessed bosses? Have you heard any of these statements about bosses in your organization?

"He never makes mistakes. Just ask him. Within fifteen minutes, he'll have figured out how it was all your fault!"

"She thinks she knows everything! Either you do it her way or not at all. If, by some miracle, you do come up with an idea she likes, by the time it's implemented she's passing it off as her own!"

"That tyrant! Hitler could have learned a thing or two from him! If anyone else tries to make a decision, he takes it as a personal insult!"

"She just put up a notice on the board! Do you believe that? When I asked her why we didn't have a meeting on it, she just said, 'Why? All they'll do is complain and ask a bunch of stupid questions!'"

"At our first meeting with him, he told us that he had been sent to clean up the place. He even told us that his nickname was 'the assassin.' That set the tone for his administration."

Do any of the above statements sound like they describe anyone you know: your current boss, or one you may have worked with in the past? You may have been telling yourself, "None of the stuff in this book is going to work with that tyrant I work for. What's the good of 'listening' to that egomaniacal north-end-of-a-horse-going-south when he only has but one thing to say: I-I-I? How can I 'give feedback' when he'll only consider it an act of insubordination? How do I 'build bridges' to someone who would see a bridge as a challenge to his authority? And how do I manage to 'care enough to confront' when such 'caring' could land me in the doghouse or the unemployment line? He's the one who ought to be reading this book!"

It is unfortunate but true that some bosses most certainly deserve the unflattering character assessments attributed to them. Managers who

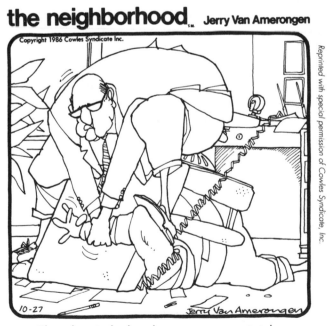

the neighborhood. Jerry Van Amerongen

Then there's the hands-on management style.

have a need to be right all the time do not respond to the normal, direct strategies we have discussed in this book.

Working with difficult bosses starts with understanding them. So preoccupied are they by their need to be right that they fail to listen even to the best suggestions. The thought that someone else might have a worthwhile idea is interpreted as a threat that someone else might be able to do their job better than they can. They may make or block decisions solely on the basis of their egos. An upper-level executive or public administrator typically has had a record of success in an environment of stability. When changes are required in order to stay competitive in a shifting marketplace or political environment, the same executive may be afraid to take risks. She has that much further to fall. And so she takes on a rigid, just-don't-forget-who's-boss stance that blocks all other input from entering the decision-making process.

No matter what the reasons for the problem may be, there are times when you have to confront your boss. Regardless of what he may believe, there are times when your boss is wrong, and you may be the only one who can tell him. There are times when the unfairness of your boss's position or policy has a direct effect on your personal integrity, and your reluctance to confront can only create additional stress and frustration for you and your staff.

You need to confront. But direct confrontations with such bosses too often result in defensive reactions followed by even more hostile attacks. Frustrated as you watch your influence deteriorate, increasingly disaffected as you fall victim to frontal attacks and less direct sabotage, you may fight back and become involved in a fruitless power struggle. You may even lose your job.

Or, you may just decide to grin and bear it, figuring you can't fight the boss. Instead of losing your job, you lose your self-respect. And when the crunch comes, your boss may yet find the way to make it your fault. After all, he's never wrong, is he? Before he'll admit to being wrong, he'll send your bags to Japan.

> Ruth Fryar was a departmental editor at Clavius Corporation, an educational publishing company. The week before the annual development meeting, she was asked by the director of development, Helen Dyson, to submit some of her ideas for the upcoming year's production. Flattered and encouraged, Ruth spent several extra hours that week preparing a list of suggestions for Helen. At the meeting, Helen presented her proposed schedule—one that included prominently some of Ruth's ideas without crediting

Ruth. Both the company president and the marketing director had good things to say about the ideas, and it was Helen who was getting all the strokes! Over lunch that day, Ruth griped about the situation to Dick Maltesi, one of the other editors. "Welcome to Clavius," Dick said. "Helen's notorious for that. Any idea anyone comes up with is her idea. Anything that goes wrong, she finds a way to blame one of us."

*　*　*　*　*　*

Art Lebold had been with Schirmer Engineering for only a few months, but he was already thinking about moving on. At Schirmer, he was realizing, there was no place to go but sideways. The boss, Dave Schirmer, was only interested in "yes men." Every time Art came up with an idea, he would hear the same expansive lecture about how Dave started the company from nothing, how Dave was recognized as an innovative leader in the industry, how the company consistently turned a profit by doing it his way. The lecturer, of course, was always Dave. Art was feeling stifled. He was making a good salary, but it was clear that there were only two ways of doing anything at Schirmer—Dave's way and the wrong way.

*　*　*　*　*　*

Rita Martinez was a promising assistant to Mike Kressen, production manager at Princess Fashions, Inc. Mike was going through a classic soap-opera divorce, and office gossip had it that he was drinking and pill-popping his way through the resulting stress. For Rita, it was an opportunity to do some independent work. Mike usually insisted on making all the decisions, but increasingly the responsibility for carrying them out was falling on Rita. She had some ideas she was sure would speed up production, but she knew that they represented a departure from Mike's way of doing things. Just to be safe, she ran them past him. "Sounds good," he said, somewhat distractedly, "but you'd better push ahead with it, or we'll be late with the fall line." Twice during the next month Rita updated Mike with verbal progress reports. "Fine, fine," he said. Rita was delighted. The work was going splendidly. She thought there might be a bonus in it for her. Then one day, Mike came screaming into her office. "What gave you the idea that you were in charge here? This is not the way we do things around here!" Rita was too shocked to argue that her way was faster and more cost-effective. She only reminded him that he had approved her plan. "What a bunch of crap!" he exploded. "I never authorized this! I've been in this business fifteen years! We never do things this way! Now we're going to have to put everyone on overtime to cover for your screw-up!"

To suggest that such bosses are extremely resistant to "upward influence" is an understatement. Yet, when an executive decision will have an impact on the customer or a manager has to do more than moan about his impossible boss, it is important for him to do his best to take the truth all the way to the top.

"For years we have been told that power corrupts and absolute power corrupts absolutely. . . . in most organizations. . . it is feeling powerless that corrupts most of all."
—**Irwin M. Rubin and David E. Berlow**

The strategies we have discussed in earlier chapters can work in such a situation. But when you're attempting to influence an ego-driven boss, they must be applied less directly and more consistently. Remember that your aim should be to influence, not to control; to win through your boss while leaving her with the feeling that she has won or that "victory" is irrelevant.

The following guidelines can help you to adapt the techniques we've been talking about to this special situation. They will work well with all bosses, but they are most crucial when dealing with the difficult bosses.

Avoid personalizing the problem.

Before you start planning how you're going to confront the boss, protect your sanity by lowering your frustration level. It's probably not your fault. When dealing with a difficult boss, many frustrated leaders tend to personalize the results: "I must be doing something wrong!" That very thought creates additional stress and frustration that will only compound the problem. Consider that your boss may be trapped by a belief in one of the myths we talked about in Chapters 1 and 2: the myth of perfection, and the myth that a "winner" must win all the time. To such a manager, anyone who suggests that he may have made a mistake represents a threat. Anyone who successfully challenges his way of doing things makes him feel like a "loser."

This is not a blanket excuse to blame your boss every time something goes wrong. If you typically have trouble with bosses and peers, maybe you ought to personalize your experience. But if you have a history of working well with others, and you see others having the same sort of problems with your boss as you do, there is no reason to blame yourself.

Do, however, hold yourself responsible for doing what you can to work harmoniously with such a boss. Try modifying your behavior in order to influence his. Changing a difficult boss is always a long shot. There is always a higher probability of changing the relationship by changing yourself.

Know and understand your boss.

Take the time to try to understand your boss and the context in which she operates. Know her goals, strengths, weaknesses, and preferred working style. Be aware of her blind spots and of the pressures she is under. At the same time, seek to understand your own psychological needs about the situation as much as you do your boss's. This way you can reasonably determine whether you can stay within your boss's comfort zone without allowing her to take you out of your own. If you have a tendency to resist authority, be aware of it before you react to your boss's bossiness. The direct, confrontational style that gets you what you want from your peers is not likely to work with your boss. Impatient ex-

From the Wall Street Journal
Permission, Cartoon Features Syndicate

"It's not really all that important that we understand each other . . . just that *you* understand *me.*

plosions about unrealistic workloads or penny-pinching budgets are unlikely to influence even the most compliant boss. If your boss won't change, you may have to. If you have reached an impasse, keep your temper in check and suggest that you break up the meeting and think about the problem for a while. When you renew the discussion, you may both have digested your differences and be able to reach an agreement.

On the other hand, you may tend to be soft-spoken and deferential toward authority. If such a style isn't getting you anywhere, it may be because your boss is someone who appreciates a good scrap. She might show more respect for your ideas if you worked at developing a forceful, assertive style of expressing them. "I want my executives to argue with me," one successful entrepreneur puts it. "I need to be convinced that they're thinking."

This is not a suggestion to become a "yes-person" on the one hand, or a conniving manipulator on the other. If staying within your boss's comfort zone brings you out of your own, you may need to hire yourself a different boss—by moving on to a new position. But before you take that step, consider frankly the extent to which you can adapt. Before you say, "That's just not me," think of the different behaviors that you have made "you" during your lifetime. Remember that driving a car was once not "you," but since it was too far to walk, you learned how. The social games involved in interpersonal relationships may once not have been "you," but since adolescence you have come to realize the benefits of learning to play them. Likewise, with your boss, you may find that you can comfortably adapt to fit rather than fight to change.

Keep listening to, and seeking clarification from, your boss until you both sense that you have achieved a mutually acceptable working relationship. If your boss remains vague or non-explicit about her expectations, take the initiative. Write down a description of your job, covering all aspects of your work and specifying what you actually spend your time doing. Take it to your boss for reaction and discussion. This can help to clarify expectations; it also informs the boss of what you really do. You will never know how effective you both can be unless you take the risk of finding out.

Keep your boss informed.

Developing and maintaining a balanced relationship with your boss means taking the initiative to keep your boss informed. Pass on any news, good or bad, that you think would be of interest to him. Don't neglect the grapevine. Your boss may not yet have discovered the benefits of MBWA. He may keep himself isolated from what's going on within the company. Avoid frivolous gossip, and make sure that rumors are passed along only as rumors. But make sure the boss knows what's going on.

Keeping a boss informed also means keeping him up-to-date on developments in his area of expertise. Take time to become an information broker for your own boss. Scan the media for pertinent articles and information. Pass them along to him for review with a friendly note: "Thought you'd be interested in the attached." Planting the seeds of information will also make him more receptive to needed changes. Most high-ego managers need to be right. As often as not, their negativity comes from insecurity. If they don't know what's happening, they are intimidated by those who do. Intimidated people are often difficult. By keeping them informed, you remove the source of their intimidation. You make it more likely that their need to be right will lead them to grab onto available data when a decision is needed. Make sure that most of that data comes from you.

Be prompt with your information, especially if it is bad news. He will find out eventually, and you do not want to give him the idea that you had been holding out on him. But convey the good news speedily as well. If you hang onto it too long, it won't be news anymore. Give him all of it—the good, the bad, and the ugly. If at all possible, include your support information and recommendations. If you've done your homework, he will appreciate it.

As important as it is to keep your boss informed, it's equally important to do it in a manner that won't cost the messenger her head, particularly when you are the messenger. Learn to time your messages for the good days; don't talk about problems when your boss is in the throes of the crisis crazies. If you must confront him on one matter, be visibly supportive on as many others as possible. Save your confrontations for the important issues; don't risk the erosion of your rapport on the corporate version of "Trivial Pursuit."

Be supportive.

Giving your candid opinions does not mean launching a crusade against the boss's authority. As a manager, you know that decisions get tougher the higher up they are made. Be prepared to support your boss in her tough decisions. Be able to disagree, but express your reservations privately, eyeball to eyeball. If you sense that you are going too far, remember the magic words that minimize the threatening effect of feedback: "I know it is your decision, and I will do all I can to implement it, but I'm concerned about. . ." Be open about expressing your opinions, but be ready to follow through with your support whatever the outcome. With such a history behind him, an Art Lebold might discover that a Dave Schirmer might be more willing to consider his ideas.

Avoid the temptation to blame the boss for an unpopular decision. Even if your people know you opposed the directive, you can still be supportive. You can say, "You're right, I do disagree. It's part of my job to express that disagreement, but it's also my job to support any decision that's made. I will act as though it were my opinion, and I expect you to do the same so that we can give it a real chance to work." Support the boss through the tough decisions, even when you disagree, and you may gain and keep her respect. You may then be able to call upon this respect when you need her support for your decisions.

Strengthen your informal, personal contacts with the boss.

Just as with colleagues and subordinates, personal contacts with your boss help build a foundation on which mutual respect can grow. Most bosses appreciate bridge building too; with difficult bosses bridge building is a necessity. Discover any mutual interests and activities you may have, and use that common ground as a starting point for conversation. Make a point of sharing any aspects of your personal life that could have an impact on the direction of your career. Such disclosures may encourage the boss to help you and may in fact provide a focus for his help. The more he understands you, your needs, and your skills, the less likely he is to offer you a promotion you do not want. (Difficult bosses hate to hear "Thanks, but no thanks" to such an offer when they are expecting gratitude.) If he knows you, he is more likely to offer you opportunities you do want.

Save such informal interaction for times when it is appropriate: at lunch, before meetings, or when the boss initiates the contact. But also take advantage of business situations to point yourself in directions you wish to go. Performance reviews can provide such an opportunity, even if your boss only goes through the motions at review time. Make him listen to your ideas. Bring up your own observations about your strengths, areas in which you feel you need additional help or experience, and directions you'd like to move in. Don't allow him to lock you into your present situation if you aren't satisfied with it. By focusing on the positive aspects of your job and conveying your enthusiasm to him, you keep your boss aware of what motivates you and of what changes will keep you motivated. Never assume that he will "just know." Remember that what your boss doesn't know is happening, isn't happening.

Finally, don't be afraid to let your boss see you as a person. Never forget the effectiveness of a congenial attitude, a greeting with a smile and a sense of humor. Don't confuse professionalism with distant serious-ness; such a style is perceived as a threat by many bosses. Learn to take advantage of unexpected, crazy events around the office to build a sense of camaraderie.

Do your job.

Of course you "do your job"; we're talking here about the subtle ad-ministrative functions that contribute to professionalism and an im-pression of maturity. Do your homework before you involve your boss in problem solving.

Even when you're dealing with a problem that must be resolved at a higher level, do everything you can to analyze all facets of the problem and be ready to present them in a well-organized manner. Keep it your boss's decision, but be prepared to help.

If you do bring a problem to your boss, be ready with prompt sugges-tions that will help to solve the problem or to prevent similar occur-rences in the future. Even when the decision is your boss's to make, she will come to see you as an asset in tackling difficult issues.

Do not try to make an important change without first running it past the boss. This comes under the category of avoiding surprises. Your boss may know something you don't. You may also be pushing an "old but-ton" that will cause her to react, not to your initiative, but to a past threat to her authority. If your boss is less than stable (like Mike Kressen, carrying the pressures of his divorce into the workplace) you may want to get written approval for any changes you want to initiate. That may save you from the situation in which Rita Martinez found herself, of not only being upbraided but being called a liar as well.

The bottom line is that job performance is still the most important requisite for success. Never get back at a difficult boss by letting the qual-ity of your work slip. Try to make your boss look good through your per-formance. At the same time, however, increase your lateral and upward visibility where possible so that you are not seen only through your boss's ineffectiveness.

Help bosses do what they do best.

Know your boss's strong points and ask him for help when it's appro-priate. As we discussed in Chapter 6, we build better rapport when we let someone help us rather than when we offer to help him. If you keep of-fering to help an ego-driven boss, you will further threaten his already fragile self-confidence. Do your job and be ready to assist, but put more energy into finding legitimate ways in which your boss can help you. By knowing his strengths, you can ask for input in areas where his ideas can serve as cornerstones for your proposals. Look for "trigger" statements, and use them: "What you said in yesterday's meeting really triggered some thoughts for me." It may be your idea, but he will be pleased to know that he provided the spark.

Recognize his effectiveness. Bosses need recognition too; and a difficult, threatened boss can absolutely crave it. Look for ways to be sincere. Don't give any recognition you don't mean. Search for compliments that you do mean, and voice them. If you give your boss legitimate support for the things he does well, your own accomplishments will appear less threatening to him.

Give bosses more than their share of credit, even when it is not entirely due.

Remember Ruth Fryar, who resented her boss's taking credit for her ideas? It is natural to feel resentful in such a situation. But it would have been more mature of Ruth and her colleagues to recognize that Helen probably didn't think of it as "stealing their ideas." She was simply making use of an organizational asset, which she, as a manager, was entitled to do. If Ruth had given Helen more of a role and some of the credit, Helen might have been able to share in Ruth's victory instead of feeling a need to steal it.

In almost any organization, a proposal with your name on it alone may be doomed to failure. Give your boss all the credit you can. Even when much or most of the work was yours, avoid being a credit hog. This is a good policy with peers and subordinates as well: "Good managers take more than their share of the blame and less than their share of the credit." Credit hogs threaten bosses and irritate colleagues. They also broadcast their lack of confidence to everyone in the organization. Visibility is important, but so is harmony. "End runs" that can make you visible without giving due credit to your boss can be hazardous to your organizational health.

Know when to give up.

Early in this book we quoted the late philosopher W.C. Fields: "If at first you don't succeed, try, try again. Then quit. Don't be a damn fool about it!" Some bosses are just not going to change their ways, even after a little creative work on your part. Some will not be capable of developing a rapport with you; others will prove to be clinically certifiable megalomaniacs who enjoy using their power to make you and everyone else feel uncomfortable. And sometimes, even with the sanest and most

"George, I like the way you handle responsibility, so I'm going to blame some things on you."

reasonable of bosses, your differences may be too great to be bridged. After a while it becomes frustrating to both of you. If you apply the principles we've outlined here and you find that your boss's ego is still cramping your style, it may be time to get out. Transfer to another department or change jobs. No one should remain in a truly intolerable situation, especially if her basic integrity is being compromised.

The art of managing your boss is often just a matter of learning to do your part in working actively with your boss. It takes two people to build a relationship based on mutual respect. But your taking the initiative may be all that is needed to smooth out a rough relationship. As we have already learned, there is never nothing you can do, only a question as to whether it will work.

In this age of collaboration, top-level performance is still the most essential requirement for success, but it is seldom enough. It is better to make your climb up any organization by building loyal and sound working relationships with bosses as well as with peers. Become a master of both for the benefit of you, your boss, and your company. Regardless of appearances, most bosses and peers are only human.

"You can't always wait for the guys at the top. Every manager at every level in the organization has an opportunity, big or small, to do something. Every manager's got some sphere of autonomy. Don't pass the buck up the line."
—Bob Anderson, Former CEO of GE

We'd love to blame our on-the-job frustrations on the fact that we don't have a wonderful leader for our CEO or boss, but Bob Anderson has the audacity to drop the ball back in our lap. It helps bring us back to the task that faces us all—making a difference where we are with what we've got. Hopefully, some of the insights in this chapter will help make that challenge easier.

QUESTIONS WORTH ASKING

"My boss hates paperwork. How do I keep him informed when he won't read my reports?"

Adjust your style of providing information to fit your boss. Peter Drucker suggests that some bosses are "readers," while others are "listeners." If your boss is a listener, ask for ten minutes to brief her in person so that she can ask you questions. You might want to write out an agenda to help the report move quickly and to have a third party write out the substance of the briefing for both of you to have on record. If your boss is a "reader," he will generally prefer to receive the report before discussing it with you. The amount of detail you provide will depend upon the boss's style, the specifics of the situation, and your mutual trust and confidence. Don't allow reports to become tedious. When written, use headings that allow your boss to scan for relevant topics, and keep entries short and concise. He can ask for additional information if he wants it.

"Should I ever go over my boss's head?"

How important is the issue? If it affects your integrity or the safety of others, and if you have attempted more direct methods of confrontation, you may make the decision to take the problem to a higher authority. Ethical issues are now in the headlines; you don't want those headlines to be your ethics. Keep in mind, however, that employees who blow the whistle must be prepared to face the consequences. Most organizations frown on an individual rocking the boat to such a degree. It's an invitation to be thrown off the boat.

Do what you can to address the problem directly first. Keep your own work above reproach and maintain a positive visibility outside of your department. Doing so may earn you an invitation to state your case to the higher-ups with no strings attached. Do your homework before you go in. Try to get the support of others who have similar concerns. Preliminary preparation will help you to determine whether the issue is worth burning all the bridges you've worked so hard to build. Then act with full knowledge that it could cost you your job; maybe even your career. In some such cases, a boat-rocker can win. In most, however, the organization will side with the boss—or send you overboard along with him. That is still no reason to sell one's soul to keep a job. That kind of job can be a living hell far worse than the stress of losing any position for the right reasons. It remains your judgment call.

KEEPERS

☐ Managing your boss is as much your job as hers.

☐ Do your part to keep information flowing, keep your boss informed.

☐ Build on common ground and search for ways to show support.

☐ Help your boss do what she does best, use her ego and her expertise.

☐ Make your boss look good; learn to serve as well as to shine.

☐ Know when to give up; your next boss may work with you instead of against you.

CHAPTER TEN

Building Empowered Teams that Meet the Challenge of Change

"Yesterday's idea of the boss, who became the boss because he or she knew one more fact than the person working for them, is yesterday's manager. Tomorrow's person leads through a vision, a shared set of values, a shared objective."

—Jack Welch, CEO of GE

I know it's hard to hear the "E" word without squirming in your chair. After all, you, like managers before you, have worked years to earn the right to manage. It's been a competitive, uphill battle and you have persevered to gain the monetary rewards and prestige you deserve. Now, you keep hearing from *experts* and executives about empowerment, self-directed teams, and the importance of teams managing themselves. This doesn't sound good for managers, and, in certain ways, you're right. They aren't shooting managers yet, but they are being asked to retire and their positions are often not being filled. Managers are being forced into extinction, and leaders at all levels are being asked to step forward. But wait! You may be saying, "I'm managing my own motivation! I'm building my bridges! I've mastered the art of balanced feedback to my team! I'm listening so well my ears are growing! I've even learned ways to manage my own boss! And now you want me to step aside?" You don't have to step aside, just step forward as an empowering leader of a team that serves their customers!

Why empowering leadership? Things they are a changin', and they are changing faster than any manager can keep up with without the committed help of his team! You can't get the quality of work required with teams *just doing their jobs!* Leaders can talk change, but it takes team members to embrace the turbulent opportunities those changes can provide. On a moving ship, anchors left in the water are not helpful. Even the best skipper goes nowhere with too many anchors clinging to the bottom. Today's only stability is stability in motion. Being stuck in the harbor isn't where effective organizations stay.

Don't forget the *imposter phenomenon*; we don't know everything! Every leader has to have people working for them that know more than he does. If he doesn't, he is in trouble. Team members must contribute their unique skills to blend together to produce winning results. That means, leaders must give up direct control of all decisions to gain true team control of the process. Empowering employees need not be a threat to today's effective leader.

> *"Moving in the direction of a partnership relationship with employees always involves two very real tensions. The first is within managers: It is the psychological struggle involved with letting go. The more we care, the stronger our vision, and the greater our self-confidence—the harder it is to let others take hold of the reins. The second tension is practical. How can we give authority and control to people who may lack the knowledge, expertise, or confidence to handle it? We cannot let the business fall apart or the customer suffer while we experiment with employee participation."*
>
> —Ken Macher

If leading your own team isn't a big enough challenge for you, try the challenge of being a part of *the bigger team*. The best leaders are "barrier busters" for change efforts within their organization. They have to know how to build and use their influence network. A team depends upon a leader's skills *and* their contacts. Now that you're sold on the importance of empowering teams, here are some guidelines worth using.

DEVELOPING AND COMMUNICATING THE VISION— LEADERS KNOW HOW TO INSPIRE TEAMS

Work your vision as a leader.

Good leaders are consistently, but constructively, corny! They actually believe their team can make a difference, and they give their team an opportunity to live up to that belief. Leaders are no better than the people on their corporate team; their teams are no better than their vision and communicated values.

> *"Creative tension comes from seeing clearly where we want to be, our 'vision,' and telling the truth about where we are, our 'current reality.' The gap between the two generates a natural tension. Creative tension cannot be generated from current reality alone. All the analysis in the world will never generate a vision. Many who are qualified to lead fail to do so because they try to substitute analysis for vision. What they never grasp is that the natural energy for changing reality comes from holding a picture of what might be that is more important to people than what is."*
>
> —Peter M. Senge, MIT Sloan School of Management

Good leaders communicate their vision in so many different ways that it's actually contagious to those around them. They don't just write it and file it; they keep referring to their vision and values repeatedly in conversation after conversation. When a mission makes a difference to a leader, it makes a difference to her team. Your challenge is to find a hundred unique, energizing ways to make your vision live in the minds of your people.

> *"I solemnly promise and declare that every customer that comes within ten feet of me, I will smile, look them in the eye, and greet them, so help me Sam."*
>
> —Sam Walton's Wal-Mart Pledge

Instead of grasping onto the crippling cynicism and powerlessness of our age, give your team members a model for personal reflection. Communicate your vision and ask, "Is this vision worthy of your commitment and support?"

Keep training a badge of adequacy.

Empowering leaders keep promoting training as a badge of adequacy for the 90s, and they prove it by participating themselves. Work to establish a cradle-to-grave commitment to job-specific training as a competitive advantage in your team's drive for quality. Care enough for your company and your team to keep everyone learning. By promoting life-long learning and cross training, you can build a team that is flexible enough to move to where the action is. Without that commitment, workers often hold on to outdated jobs and resist even needed changes. Victims are hard to motivate; life-long learners are opportunists that can grasp changes as a welcome challenge. Only when intelligence permeates the entire organization can decision making and creative initiative be fully decentralized. If there is no learning, there is no empowerment.

"We're convinced that as technology becomes more and more accessible to more and more competitors, companies like Xerox are going to compete not on the basis of who has the best technology, but on who has the best people. And training and developing the best people will increasingly be a competitive weapon."

—**David Kearns**

Training does more than develop new skills. It also provides a forum for allowing the healthy discharge of frustration that's a byproduct of change. It provides a place for clarification and performance checks to occur, and helps break teams out of the stagnation of the status quo. When any team rests too long, they rust. Invest at least five percent of your time and your team's time in training.

Be ready to ask frequently:

What training do we need to help our team meet our objectives and stay ahead of the competition?

What three things did you learn from that program that are worth sharing with other members of our team?

What would it take for our team to understand the system well enough to make local decisions by ourselves?

Earn and keep the trust of your team.

Integrity is back in! Leaders who don't have any are having their bags sent to Japan, or they are keeping their bags and taking them to jail. Trust is a fragile commodity that is important to maintain, easy to lose, and hard to win back. Know your code of conduct and the values you stand for as a leader, and then work in good faith to keep your code. Don't be afraid to be yourself; it is one of the best kept secrets of being an effective leader. You will engage your team when you are authentic. As a handy guideline for you and your people, remember: "If you wouldn't want to explain it on *60 Minutes*, don't do it!" Leaders don't wait for forced compliance; they take the high ground and build new opportunities there! Empowering leaders walk their talk!

> *"I don't think you can grow a company successfully unless you are able to grow personally. That is what we mean by 'company.' Compagna implies breaking bread together, and, in the end, what could be more fundamental or important? Simplistic but true. Why are we here on earth? What am I doing? Who benefits from this? These are valid questions for business people to ask—and answer, with no words over three syllables and no business terms. You can't add value unless you have values."*
> —Paul Hawken, Smith & Hawken

If leaders don't talk about and act on their values, they shouldn't expect those who work for them to act on theirs. Russ Walden, President of Ridgecrest Properties, has developed a unique way to communicate his values and build trust. He likes to limit his business philosophy to one page. For Russ, anything more would be boring and unlikely to be read. He uses it to communicate his personal code to everyone he works with. With new hires, he gives the sheet for each to read, saying, "You don't have to follow this, but it's important for you to understand that I will." Here's a sample of the entries on Russ Walden's page:

Russ Walden's list of mostly true and mostly plagiarized thoughts on the management process (in no particular order):

- A person may be appointed to high position, but never to leadership. Leaders are effective only through the authority conferred on them by those upon whom they depend for results.

- Leaders produce consent; others seek consensus.

- Manage a business by its economics, not by the accounting numbers.

- It is better to be approximately right than precisely wrong.

- Ethics are non-negotiable.

- The personal dignity of each individual is inviolate. A manager who often breaks this rule will eventually self-destruct, but I will probably get him (or her) first.

- As a manager, ask yourself, "How would I like it if my boss treated me the way I treat those who work for me? " If you are unsure, read Luke 6:31.

- Authority is not inherently useful, but you can greatly influence most of the things which you cannot directly control. A manager without influence is a contradiction of terms.

- Create real values and the earnings will follow. Never sacrifice tomorrow's values for today's reportable earnings.

- A person has a right to know the significance of his work.

- We will only do things of which we can be proud. If our people are ashamed of a project it will be a disaster.

- If you aren't having fun in your work, fix the problem before it becomes serious; ask for help if you need it. If you can't fix it and won't ask for help, please go away before you spoil the fun for the rest of us.

- Never let well enough alone.

- Build some regular customer contact into the job of every person in the company.

- Defending yesterday is far more risky than making tomorrow.

- Manners are the lubricating oil of organizations.

Russ Walden not only wrote his page; he lived it. He once fired a top sales manager just before opening a new development because the man had abused a temporary worker. The statement on his page about the personal dignity of each individual being "inviolate" said nothing about the timing, the position, or the sales implications of the person involved. To the shock of many in the company, Russ fired his most productive sales manager over the incident. He was rewarded years later when talking to a customer. When asked why he had come to this particular development, he reported having a friend whose wife had been supported when the sales manager was fired. The client said, "Any company that would support their people that way, certainly will take care of my parents if they live here." It does pay to walk your talk! What would you want on your page? To maintain the trust of your team, be prepared to back up what you write.

Share information freely.

If you want innovation and synergistic teamwork, you can't have total control of information. Make a choice! Without information there is no team empowerment. Give timely, focused information to all your people and innovation and productivity will follow. That which will eventually be revealed should be immediately revealed to allow early course-corrections and effective team brainstorming. There are numerous reasons to be cautious about sharing information; some are even legitimate. Yet none outweighs the advantages of open communication.

> *"I hate bosses who distance themselves from people. We have*
> *no secrets here. So what if information gets to the competition?*
> *The organization can only be as good as the amount of*
> *information shared among people."*
> —Karl Krapek, President of Otis Elevator Co.

By sharing information freely, you keep it working for you. Even when you are not thinking about a problem, your team will be thinking for you. Treat information and facts as friends, and let your team and stake holders get to know your friends.

Sharing meaningful information is not flooding people with unnecessary facts and stacks of paper to add to their already overwhelming piles. Don't make up in quantity of pages what you lack in useful, targeted information. Information overload enrages instead of empowers! Never let information or controls choke or strangle your people, or they will send your bags to Japan or worse.

> *"I can't stand this proliferation of paperwork. It's useless to*
> *fight the forms. You've got to kill the people producing them."*
> —Vladimir Kabaidze, General director of the
> Ivanovo Machine Building Works, Moscow

Information not only promotes innovation, it sets the stage for change by helping to build awareness of the need to change. People change best when they are dissatisfied with where they are. Sometimes there are complaints, and the need for a change is obvious and well received when announced. You've heard workers say, "It's about time. We should have done this years ago." Such changes are easy to initiate at that point, but few will thank their leadership for taking so long to act.

Some needs are less obvious because they are not yet evident to your team. Early information on the need for change is critical when leaders in any way expect people to be surprised by a change. Progressive leaders take the time to build a case from their team's perspective that will make them aware of how things could be better and how it will get worse if something is not done. Early information, meetings, and discussions about the need will help get your team on board for any change.

Know the people that depend upon you for information; know on whom, in turn, you depend. If you don't get the information you or your team needs, it's time to reread Chapter 9. Remember, what information you consistently ask for you will get. Be persistent and focused on information that will make a difference in your team efforts. If you don't know what information your team needs, ask them, "What information do you need to do your job?"

Use friendly controls.

Leaders give more than information; they give their teams meaningful ways to keep score. What gets measured and looked at gets done. True facts and financial controls are liberating. They let people focus on the winning activities that make a difference on their mission and their bottom line. Team members truly know if they are making a difference, because their leaders give them ways to follow the action.

> *"Our management system is based on the premise that business is essentially a game—one, moreover, that almost anyone can learn to play. As with most games, however, people won't bother to learn it unless they get it. That means, first, they must understand the rules; second, they must receive enough information to let them follow the action; and third, they must have the opportunity to win or lose. That's exactly how this company is run. Every week the department heads hold a meeting at which they go over the income statement, comparing actual performance with monthly goals. Each department goes back and does the same thing with the*

*supervisors who repeat the process with the workers on the
shop floor. From top to bottom, people in this company really
do understand what the business is about."*

—Bo Burlingham, CEO
Springfield Remanufacturing Center Corp.

Keep data on the important measurements and graph them to keep
them visible to your people. Learn to "red flag" key indicators to initiate
early problem solving. Refer to your measurements frequently. Without
meaningful measurements it is easy for teams and leaders to mistake activity or information for achievement.

Howard Osterizer Health Organization was referred to affection-
ately by those in the community as "HOHO for health". But all
was not "HOHO" between departments. Problems in government
and insurance funding along with costly compliance guidelines
had caused one administrator to confess that "here in the South,
DRG's means 'Dah Revenue's Gone'." Head nurse, Crystal
Gaglegreen, and Fred Frei, hospital materials manager, had not
found the humor in the hospital's predicament. They were known
hospital wide for their quarterly budget free-for-alls over "unnecessary costs." Tired and bruised by the latest war, Fred decided to
try a dose of "Frei" information to break the stalemate. He focused
on one of the principal problem areas, linen costs on Crystal's
floor. He went to her station waving a white flag on a stick. Her
warm smile and noticeable but subtle chuckle indicated the recep-
tivity needed for a possible breakthrough. He took the offensive in
a pleading tone, "I'm tired of our quarterly battle. I want a truce,
and I think I've come up with a way to make one last. We battle
every three months over numbers we can do nothing about; the
quarter is always over. Linen costs are always one of the major
problems. If you are interested, I'd like to get your linen costs numbers to you every week so you can monitor your floor's own numbers." Crystal was unaware that his computer could even do that.
Fred confessed, "It can't, but I can have our people figure it out and
graph it for you by hand until we can find a way for the computer
to do it for us." Fred's colorful graph of linen costs found a prominent location on the nurse's station wall. It was visible, and it
made a difference. At HOHO, Frank and Crystal turned it around
to HOHUM!

You may not have to do your record keeping by hand. For those that take the time to master them, computerized systems can provide new ways to stay close to the vital signs of any organization. Emerging ESS (Executive Support Systems) software systems provide electronic mail, on-line targeted news services and, most significantly, a nearly seamless interface between the leader's desktop and the company's mainframe. The system targets the right activity and the right facts and gives you graphic portrayal of key company success factors and competitor data. You can see trends emerging, opportunities arising, and problem areas pulsating in red. Such friendly facts and congenial controls remove team decision-making from the realm of mere opinion. The computer revolution has been fought, and the computer has won. If you haven't gotten on board, start introducing yourself and your team to the victor.

Focus your time, forms, and measurements on the factors that let your team win and win big. Find out what's profitable and serves the customer and what's not; do more of the former and less of the latter.

Give freedom within limits.

For Robert Waterman, author of *The Renewal Factor*, empowerment is another word for "directed autonomy." Empowerment is never total freedom; it is choices within established boundaries.

> *"People in every nook and cranny of the organization are empowered—encouraged in fact—to do things their way. Suggestions are actively sought. But this all takes place within a context of direction. People know what the boundaries are; they know where they should act on their own and where not. The boss knows that his or her job is to establish, and then truly get out of the way."*
>
> —Robert H. Waterman

Give adequate thought to your boundaries. Where are your limits to team empowerment? Be tight where you are not willing to allow choices and loose where you want to foster innovation, commitment, and empowerment. Within your boundaries, learn to guide but don't over control. Set direction but not detailed strategy. Your latest strategic planning is great as long as you don't take it too seriously. Write your strategies in pencil encouraging frequent opportunity for adjustment. Have a big safety net under your people who make mistakes in the midst of their heroic efforts. You're a leader, and leaders are there to support their team.

> *"You must provide a framework in which people can act. For*

example, we have said that our first priority is safety, second is punctuality, and third is other services. So, if you risk flight safety by leaving on time, you have acted outside the framework of your authority. The same is true if you don't leave on time because you are missing two catering boxes of meat. You give people a framework, and within that framework you let people act."

—Jan Carlzon, CEO SAS

Provide a safety net for legitimate mistakes, but don't forget to confront persistent problems. Take a second look at Chapter 4. Know your eight thousand-foot level, the point where you participate in the failure of your team by not holding team members accountable for consistent poor performance. Some people don't seem to want to be empowered; they want to be adopted. No team will emerge when some team members are carried instead of being challenged to contribute. You will still need to confront your resident anchors; get them on board or cut them off before they drag the ship down with them.

Working smart in a high quality/cost containment world.

Keep your team focused on priority changes. Change is here to stay, but the costs can be high for your team if you don't manage and pace the change process. Never put change on a pedestal. It is not a cure-all, and it's not always necessary. It is always costly. Keep people abreast of existing priority work so that changes can be timed to keep pace with established demand cycles. True innovation is a marriage between what is needed and what is possible. In a changing world, time is at a premium. Make frequent checks on priority to keep your team working smart.

Develop a *scrounger mentality* on your team. Learn from the mission of *the scrounger* from the movie, *The Great Escape*. Their mission was clear: assist the Allied effort by helping POW's escape to occupy as many German soldiers in recapturing them as possible. James Garner played the role of *the scrounger*; he was to beg, barter, and innovatively steal or create everything needed to mobilize the mission. Now that's exciting—a significant mission and no budget! He had to make quality happen without throwing money at it. Does that sound familiar to you?

"Lack of planning on your part does not constitute a crisis on my part."
—**Sign used by Peter Ueberroth before the 1984 Olympics**

Getting quality and service excellence does not always mean more money; it means a creative commitment to get the right job done right. That means all team members must work smart on real priorities and initiate early problem solving when there is too much to do. Stress the need to *both* take initiative *and* do priority shifts in keeping team members in their peak productivity zone.

Don't leave any worker in the **drone zone**! They may be moving, but they certainly aren't producing. Whether you inherited people who have encamped there or you've let people slip into it because you don't trust the quality of their work, don't let people stay there! Let your drones learn the secret of initiative. If they take initiative, you won't have to manage them; they will be managing themselves. What's in it for your drones? It's simple; they get to enjoy their day and spend less time dealing with you. Keep them focused on the four Ts of initiative— *Tell me* when you have time to help, *Take action* when your action supports our mission, *Train* for the future needs of the team, and, if you do all three, you will have my *Trust.* You not only need to be trusted as a leader, you need to train your people on how important it is for them to earn and keep your trust.

Once team members have earned your trust, work to keep theirs by not overloading them with too much work. It's too easy to move your team right through their peak productivity zone into their **panic zone**. In the age of quality, you don't want any worker juggling too many responsibilities and settling for less than doing the job right. No team can do it all; you want them to focus on the right work. Let every team member know that you insist on "no surprises." Use the Four Xs Rule—"For every unit of time you may be late on any responsibility, give four times the warning to me and other team members."

When inadequate resources are available and significant work is not getting done, be a professional pest in communicating your teams needs up the organization. Teams must work together to find the best ways to use limited organizational resources, and they need your help when their objectives are unrealistic.

To keep your team working smart, ask your now familiar one-on-one questions frequently:

Are there any red flags?

What are your principal priorities?

What do you need from me to get the job done?

Don't just be enthusiastic—generate enthusiasm.

Most people want to be enthusiastic about their work. It takes more than painting a picture of the vision and preaching the mission statement. It takes leaders who are able to kindle that same fire in the eyes of their workers. Being overly enthusiastic may not be the answer; overly enthusiastic leaders with no connection to reality tend to produce a predictable response from the vast majority of us—nausea! It's okay to believe in your company and your people and to show it, but there is more to leadership than being enthusiastic. The difference between being enthusiastic and generating enthusiasm is whose ideas you get excited about. Be as excited about other team members' ideas as you are about your own. Learn to search for, find, listen to, and reflect back pockets of enthusiasm whenever you find it in the eyes and actions of your team. Energetic, enthusiastic listening is your best tool to energize them.

"I consider my ability to arouse enthusiasm among my people the greatest asset I possess, and the way to develop the best that is in a person is by appreciation and encouragement."
—**Charles Schwab, CEO of Charles Schwab**

A good leader respects the value of the ideas her team can generate. Consider yourself more a prospector than a wise sage. Every time you walk the halls and talk to your people pretend you are mining for gold—the golden ideas, energy and commitment that you find in the people you work with. Be able to say, "You're excited about that, aren't you! Tell me more." As you probe for more information and reflect back their energy through your own eyes, be ready to take the gold to the bank: "That's a great idea. Would you mind sharing that in the staff meeting this afternoon? I think we can all learn something from this!" Soon you will find the enthusiasm where it belongs, in the minds and hearts of the people who have to make it happen. Let their commitment and values be as contagious as yours.

Take time to ask these one-on-one questions frequently:

What's working for you?

What are you doing differently?

What's producing results for you?

Be accessible and build team morale.

Empowering leaders put their calendar where their mouth is; they spend time talking to their people! Good leaders often invest up to twenty-five to thirty percent of their time in building attitude, morale, and motivation within their team network. You learned the importance of bridge building in winning over even the most difficult enemy. In building teams, the bridge building creates the bonding that is necessary to forge a committed work unit.

> *"I . . . walk around and see my people, because just to walk around and dare to be strong, dare to give, is much more valuable than any decision I could make or any report I could read. What I give away then is mental health to the organization. The most unproductive time we have is when we sit at our desks. Because the only thing we do is read history: what has already happened, what we cannot do anything about. When we leave our offices and start to walk around and talk to people, that's when we make things happen. You give your thoughts; you get thoughts back; you draw conclusions; perhaps you even make decisions."*
>
> —Jan Carlzon, CEO SAS

Listen, listen, listen! Your listening lets your people know that you are there to serve not just to direct. Let them teach you what they know and what they need.

Support, support, support! When empowering leaders are *on their rounds*, they give team members more than their share of the credit and take most of the heat for problems generated in the pursuit of team goals.

Create a culture of pride that recognizes the effectiveness of your team members. Take the time to recognize and formally acknowledge your workers and other departments and people who make needed change possible. Keep the team the hero. If you make the change theirs, they will work to reach new heights. If you allow any one person to hog the credit, the others who helped make it happen may just choose to let it die.

Train your team to be professional pests for needed change.

It doesn't take a leader to move people to fix something that's obviously broken. It takes a leader to inspire comfortable winners to move to a higher ground! What are you doing to help your people make the paradigm shifts that will move your group productively on a journey into the future. No leader worth her salt, will settle for trying to maintain the status quo. In today's world of change and global competition, defending the status quo is another way of greasing your slide into the corporate graveyard.

> *"We need a department of surprises. Whatever we do, we have to preserve the sense of being different. Otherwise, the time will come when everyone who works for us will say The Body Shop is just like every other company. It's big. It's monolithic. It's difficult. This is going to be a huge company in a few years. We just have to make sure we won't wind up like an ordinary company."*
> —Anita Roddick, founder and managing
> director of The Body Shop

Every leader needs to keep their team out of their comfort zone and hooked on the goal of continuous process improvement. Who is taking care of the department of surprises for your company?

Help promote innovative changes throughout your organization. If you lead a team and you want your people to give you their innovative ideas, ask for it regularly by encouraging and honoring diversity. Be open to the unconventional, and be relentless in promoting fresh eyes to uncover needed changes and new opportunities.

This is not a call for total change. Every improvement is a result of change. Every change is not an improvement. Leave some of the culture intact as a familiar anchor to help teams weather through the storms of change. People in the midst of change need something familiar to hold on to. It's another manifestation of the high tech/high touch paradox. As we race into the future, we grasp fondly for the things of the past that give us some hope of continuity. Let your people keep the things worth keeping, but discourage and confront passive, nonassertive clinging to the status quo whenever you see it.

Remember the importance of using resistance from Chapter 8. In our constantly changing world, team resistance goes with the territory. Most decisions that bring about changes are seldom black and white, they are more or less workable. Attempts at threatening, silencing, or otherwise avoiding team criticism of change will only force the resistance underground into the restrooms, lounges, and cafeterias. It may also increase the likelihood of your own people sabotaging even good changes. Teams have been known to send whole proposals to Japan!

If you want your people to give you the truth, ask for it regularly. With costly and hard to reverse decisions, if early consensus forms, make sure that you have one person prepared to express an alternative

ALL THOSE OPPOSED - SIGNIFY BY SAYING, " I QUIT !! "

point of view. It's too easy for critical discussion to stop when early agreement occurs. It's hard for any leader to be open to negative comments, but that's exactly what helps to minimize it's impact. Keep your own "hotline" open to those involved in your world of change. Make learning to disagree without being disagreeable a team goal. Then, be open and nondefensive. Remember, listening makes listeners.

Find the winning balance—help your team make a living and a life.

Take time to invest in the long-term sanity of your team. The evidence is clear: find balance in your life or lose your vitality on the job. You might be saying, "Now, I know you've gone mad. You can't have time for a a balanced life and be a good team player!" Wrong! You can prove it yourself. When you buy tickets to a play or a pivotal playoff game, do you act differently on the job? If you are like most, you get there early and go right to work on things you have to get done. When long-winded, professional visitors try and establish squatters rights in your visitor's chair, you intervene: "Can't talk! I've got tickets. Suck air somewhere else!" When your boss arrives, you seek her out. Your opening line is predictable, "I've got tickets." You quickly ask for a list of the things you have to get done. When people call, you quickly say, "I've got tickets. I've got to leave right at five o'clock. Now, what do you need from me?" You get the picture. You know the end of the story; you complete a tremendous amount of work, and you leave at five o'clock. The secret of life is simple—have tickets every day.

> *"In our fast lane lifestyles, more and more of us are looking for the off-ramps. Even if you win the rat race, you're still a rat. There is a powerful undercurrent of nostalgia for simple relationships."*
>
> —David M. Zach

Stay focused on the job and resist the temptation to waste time when you are there. Make dates with your family and other "energy boosters!" Take three daily stress breaks on the job by taking a walk out of your work area or reading a novel. Take time for regular exercise, a walk with your dog, and an occasional good comedy. All can do wonders to help you avoid burnout in the competitive 90s. But never forget that there is more to life than finishing today's version of a critical crisis. Neither you or any of your team members would want placed on their tombstone, "He finished everything on his to-do-list."

> *"Why doesn't dad have time to play with me at night?" "He's been promoted and that means more work honey." "Well, why don't they put him in a slower group?"*
>
> —Ed Foreman

QUESTIONS WORTH ASKING

"With the renewed emphasis on quality and TQM, how do you make sure you can keep quality and still promote needed innovation and risk taking?"

I have my own guiding philosophy that sums up the delicate balancing act required in stretching the envelope of innovation through the mistakes such risks require while still maintaining legendary quality in customer service. It's simpler than it sounds. Support a team attitude that redefines quality at different phases of product or service development. Support your team making their mistakes early in the development process and away from the public, while doing the right things right the first time with a customer, just in time, all the time, at minimal cost, maximum speed, and maximal customer satisfaction. And, oh yes, keep things moving by doing it better again forever! It's not impossible, just exciting. Keep your team focused on embracing the ongoing challenge of change.

"What is your definition of empowerment?"

Rosabeth Moss Kanter argues that teams need three basic "power tools" for people to experience empowerment. They need information, resources, and leadership support. I would agree. But for me, empowerment is something more; people experience it in a personal way. Empowerment is the process of enabling employees to be committed, concerned, and involved. They feel they make a difference and they do. I would add, that long before the word empowerment had burst onto the management training horizon, the experience of empowerment had already existed in the minds of many successful leaders and teams.

Does this experiment in empowerment and self-managed teams mean I won't be making any decisions as a manager?

The kind of decisions you make will change. Much more of your time will be spent keeping the mission and vision alive, deciding who needs to be involved, clarifying team boundaries, deciding what coalitions to build, what information to share, and what measurements to keep. Orchestra conductors still get to pick the music. You'll spend more time deciding how to get what your people need to make sure your team's music soars to new heights.

KEEPERS

☐ Work your vision and values.

☐ Keep training a badge of adequacy for you and your team.

☐ Walk your talk and earn the trust of your team every day.

☐ Provide timely, focused information early.

☐ Use friendly controls that let your team follow the score that counts.

☐ Define your boundaries before you empower.

☐ Use initiative, priority shifts, and the Four Xs rule to keep your team working smart.

☐ Mine your team's pockets of enthusiasm and innovation.

☐ Develop a department of surprises with a team of professional pests.

☐ Work at making a living and a life by having tickets every day.

CHAPTER ELEVEN

Making This Book Worth Buying: The Challenge of Self-Change

"Like the invisible garments in 'The Emperor's New Clothes,'
actual behavior change on the job is largely an illusion.
Indeed, relapse rates can be as high as ninety percent."
— W.R. Rodgers

So now you're set. You're ready to charge out and confront any situation your job may throw at you. You have some new tools to prevent conflict from arising, to deal with it promptly and assertively when it does arise, and ultimately to make it work for you. All it will take to apply the strategies and techniques presented in this book are a few changes in your personal style. Nothing to it but to do it. Right?

"And then, and then. . . and then, and then. . . and then, and
then . nothing."
— Haitian carnival song

Well . . . self-change can't be that easy, can it? Otherwise there wouldn't be so many bitter jokes about New Year's resolutions. We all have our dreams of a "new us." We all have made resolutions of self-change at one time or other. But for most of us, sustaining real change is significantly more difficult than having a dream or a resolution. If it were easy, you probably would not have bothered reading this book. You would have made the changes after the last book, or the last training video, or the last seminar. How long did your resolve to change stay with you then? Three, four days? A week? Probably not much longer than that, if you're like most of us. But the fact that you picked up this book is a strong indication that you were not ready to give up.

We've all made resolutions that faded into failure, but it doesn't have to be that way. This final chapter will help you make it more likely that three months from now, these strategies and techniques discussed will have become part of your own management style.

"When you're through changing, you're through."

—Bruce Barton

Self-change is possible; in fact, you can't stop it. You have been changing throughout your life, and you will continue changing until you die. You have learned, unlearned, and relearned many things in your pursuit of mastery over your world.

Some of us try to hold on to past habits by trying to convince ourselves that we are hopelessly stuck in the past. We say to ourselves, "That's just the way I am." The variations on this theme are endless: "You can't teach an old dog new tricks!" "You can't beat the system." "You can't fight city hall." Or, in Popeye's version, "I yam what I yam what I yam." They are illusions. Such statements may keep us from taking risks, but they also fail to address the fact that we do choose to change when it is beneficial for us to do so and when little conscious effort is required. We are, in fact, changing all the time. The you of today is not the you of five years ago.

"Life is change; that's how it differs from the rocks."

—John Wyndham

Too often our problems with directed self-change arise from the fact that we generally try to change everything all at once. We forget that the world imposes so many demands on us that we have only so much time and energy to devote to the process of change. It is hard work. No matter how sincere we may be, our half-hearted and ill-planned efforts to change in many areas at once quickly dissipate in the harsh reality of today's world. After a few days, we slide back into doing things the way we always have. Our loved ones, friends, and co-workers almost expect it of us. They are reassured by it; they support our conviction that true self-change is just not possible. "Well," you tell yourself, "I can't change, and this proves it. I'm just the way I am."

Nonsense.

What you want to change we will leave up to you. This chapter provides guidelines for making the changes happen. No matter what changes you want to make, if you internalize these guidelines, self-change can become a reality.

> *"Habit is habit, and not to be flung out of the window by any man, but to be coaxed down the stairs one step at a time."*
>
> —Mark Twain

Focus your efforts on specific goals.

Manage yourself the way you hope to manage others. Self-change starts with spending time on self-awareness. You must make the decision to change, concentrate on acting differently to effect the change, see yourself doing it over time, and use your successes to keep your momentum going in support of the change. The busy, demanding lives we lead leave us only so much time for such self-awareness. For this reason, it's a good idea to limit yourself to three central areas of change at any one time.

In reviewing the material in this book, take some time to narrow your focus. You may want to make a quick review of the "keeper" statements at the end of each chapter. Select three specific areas in which you most

" GOOD MORNING, EXERCISE LOVERS!..."

want to change. For example: "I'm going to care enough to consistently confront Old Charlie, my 'resident anchor.' I'm going to focus on problem solving instead of always telling my people what they're doing wrong. I'm going to be more positive and 'build bridges' to Lois in accounting." Consider that you will have the best success at making changes that you truly want to make. Don't take on changes that you're reluctant to make simply because someone else thinks you ought to make them.

Then get even more specific. Ask yourself, "How do I want to be handling these problems three months from now? What will I actually be doing differently? How much time will I need to invest in effecting the changes?" Allow yourself time to actually visualize yourself as the "new you." Build a detailed mental picture of yourself as you would choose to be.

If you like your visualized image of yourself as a changed person, if you can actually see yourself acting differently, you have accomplished the first step in making change possible. You have established your three clear goals.

Break down each of your goals into specific small steps.

Once you have focused on a goal, it is necessary to break it down into a series of attainable steps that will make success more likely. One of the surest ways to abort an effort toward change is to take on an impossible goal that assures a quick and ignominious failure. Then, when you fail, you use your failure as evidence that change is impossible. "That proves it—it's just the way I am." Right? Wrong! When you were learning to drive a car, did you start out by trying to qualify for the Indianapolis 500? Unless you wanted to commit suicide, I doubt it. If you played tennis in high school and you wanted to take up the game again, you wouldn't start out by challenging Boris Becker to a set? If you wanted to lose seventy pounds, would you try to do it all in a week on a fad diet of celery, bean curd, tofu, and a cantaloupe? Of course not! You would last three days and then be assaulted by a three-pound bag of Oreo cookies at the supermarket. You'd eat the entire bag to provide conclusive proof that you had no willpower at all: "I guess diets just aren't for me. I was born to eat Oreos."

"Effective companies are not built on any one strategy but on incremental moves. There are a thousand things done a tiny bit better; it's the 'three yards and a cloud of dust.' Incremental change is the only kind of change that exists."

—Peters and Waterman

Effective self-change starts off with realistic steps. Establish an initial step for each goal you focus on. Make it something you can do within the first week to get started on the road to change; something specific, attainable, and easily accomplished. We start in the parking lot, not the race track. We hit the tennis ball around with our spouse, not Boris Becker. We try changing one eating habit and lose a pound a week.

A woman I met at a seminar told me about her most successful effort at self-change. She had been stuck working for a boss whose jeering sexism was both thwarting her career and compromising her integrity. When she confronted him about his excluding her from the decision-making process, his reply was, "All the real decisions around here are made at the urinals, honey!" Several times she had been ready to quit. Finally, she took the step of writing a letter to company headquarters to document the problem—and to submit her resignation. But before she mailed it, she decided to make an effort at bridge building, step by step. First, she made a point of stopping by his office to sincerely compliment him on the new marketing campaign. Within a week, after learning that he was a tennis buff, she caught him as he was leaving one afternoon and struck up a conversation about tennis on the way to the parking lot. She looked for cartoons that could make him laugh at his own sexism and sent him one with a note saying, "This reminded me of you. Thought you'd enjoy." He seemed to like her banter and actually began to initiate contact himself. She continued her efforts by asking him for his input on one of her projects. By then he had begun to temper his comments and, more importantly, to listen to her ideas and to give her interesting projects to work on. After three months, she tore up her letter of resignation.

Share your commitment with someone else.

One of the best strategies for effecting change is to tell someone else about your commitment. There is ample evidence that sharing the commitment increases the likelihood of fulfilling it. Alcoholics Anonymous, Smokenders, diet groups, church and synagogue self-help groups all operate on this principle. Important changes are hard to work on alone, and privately held goals are notoriously easy to cheat on.

Enlist some support in your struggle to become a more effective manager. Choose someone you trust and whom you see often, whether it is a friend, a family member, or a business associate. (You may even want to make it your boss; who would be more motivated to help you become a better leader?)

Do not be embarrassed about enlisting help. If you choose your partner well, he or she will probably be honored to be chosen.

Tell your partner about the specific changes you're trying to make. Ask for his help, but don't bore him with a long list. Stay focused on your three goals. Let him know that you expect the process to be difficult at times; old habits have a way of creeping back in. Ask him to remind you if he sees evidence of old habits returning. But also request his recognition and support when he catches you changing. Recognition of your efforts and your success from someone you care about will help keep you on the path toward change. You may want to involve him further by arranging to celebrate together some preestablished milestone in the change process.

Give yourself specific deadlines for your changes, and make your partner aware of these deadlines. We talked about this strategy in our discussion of procrastination, and it is equally applicable here. Long-range goals have a tendency to fall by the wayside because of the daily tasks that seem to take precedence even though they may not be as important. Your partner can keep you focused on the long-range goal of change by keeping you mindful of your deadlines.

It is especially important to choose someone who will motivate you. Don't pick a "Lucy" (a negative, dreary person who will sap your energy). Choose someone who will boost your energy; who will celebrate with you instead of pulling you down. You, of course, are your own most powerful motivator, but it can be of tremendous help to have someone pulling for you in the change process. Self-change is a noble and individual challenge, but it can be made much easier by the support of others around you.

Some leaders take the added step of forming in-house support groups. They meet once a month over lunch to share information, insights, and reflections gathered from experiences and reading. One manager said of his support group, "That group is my corporate Jewish mother! It makes me feel guilty when I don't take time to read. If you promise to change, you don't go back until you do."

Your co-workers will need to be conditioned to your new self as well. Some may be naturally skeptical about your self-change. The only thing that will remove their skepticism is a history of new behavior. They will become aware of your attempts to change, however, if you let them in on it. This will put you in the conspicuous position of having to put up or shut up, but it will also increase the likelihood that you will put up. It gives others the opportunity to look, find evidence, and begin to accept the fact that you are indeed dealing with conflict in a new set of ways.

HERMAN®

© 1985 Universal Press Syndicate

3 9

"Get down before you hurt yourself."

Post signs to remind yourself of your commitment to change.

Even the most sincere commitment to change can be sabotaged by habit. How quickly we can forget our goals and go back on automatic pilot! Signs along the highway are designed to catch your attention and to tell you what to expect up ahead. Such signs make you aware of your choices. Use the same concept to prompt your efforts to change.

Use signs to remind yourself of the changes you're trying to effect. Write key words such as, POSITIVE FEEDBACK; BETTER LISTENING; PROCRASTINATION! on one of those colorful stickers and put it on your office telephone. You will be reminded of your commitment every time you make a call. Put similar reminders on your checkbook, on the dashboard or sun visor of your car, on your refrigerator at home, on your TV set. One manager who attended one of my seminars placed her reminders on the wall facing the toilet in her condo, where she knew she would see and study it several times a day. The more out-of-the-ordinary the location, the more effective the cue. Keep in mind that you must change the messages frequently whenever you catch yourself not noticing them any more, or they will lose their effectiveness.

One company I know of has designated one of its secretaries as "tickle specialist." Any employee who wished to be reminded of a particular self-change goal on a given date files the information with her. As part of her job, she designs and sends personalized reminder notes at the designated times. It works!

Your calendar can be the best self-change reminder you have. A great saying framed on the wall soon drifts into the gray attic of unseen treasures, but you look at your calendar every day. When you have established your three goals, write your three key words on a Post-it note (an invention ranking with the computer as one of the most useful of our time). Place it on your calendar as a reminder. The yellow on white provides a good eye-scan focus. Read your key words before you start each day. At the end of the day, write one thing you did to bring yourself closer to your goals. Then move it to the next day. Follow this procedure for a month before changing your goals. Long-range goals seldom get onto your daily calendar to-do list unless you put them there. There is evidence that looking at and thinking about your targeted areas of change for a month can begin the process of internalizing it as a new habit. Use your signs to keep yourself aware of changes you want to make. Change becomes easier when you are aware of the choices you must make to get yourself there.

Condition yourself to your "new self."

A plant that has sprouted and begun to grow will die if it is not nurtured by the elements. It needs sun, water, and nutrients from the soil. Likewise, if you do not nurture your change, it may die on the vine before you can fully incorporate it into your personal behavior pattern. Don't expect the process of change to take care of itself once it has been initiated. It seldom happens that way. The work environment contains too many distractions.

Find and develop the mental ammunitions that will nurture the process of change. For a start, reread this book. If you haven't underlined the key passages that relate to your desired areas of change, do so the next time you read it. Underline like crazy. Whenever you read another book or article, listen to a tape, or attend a seminar relating to your areas of desired change, make a note of the most relevant and stimulating passages. It is natural to be fired up and motivated on such first readings or hearings. Take some time to reexpose yourself to such material at regular intervals. Don't overdo it, but do invest a certain amount of time each week to reading, viewing, or listening to material that will support your changes.

Put any materials on self-change that you find to be particularly useful into a "keeper" notebook and review it periodically. Reread the key quotes and summary statements every few months to keep yourself reminded of your goals and your progress. A good time to review these keepers is when you're on hold on the telephone.

Some managers record their keepers and key quotes on audio tape, interspersed with their favorite musical selections. They keep the tapes in their car and play them whenever they're stuck in traffic. Every year they add a new tape to their collection. The old tapes we play on our built-in tape recorders in the brain are seldom erased. We spend too little time replaying our past victories, inspirational quotes, and our training keepers. They tend to fade quickly from our short-term memories because we don't go back and replay them. Make a choice about which of your tapes you want to replay.

A systems analyst at a public utility company used his computer skills to come up with a unique system of recording and reviewing his keepers. He wrote a program that stored and randomly flashed his key reminders in a corner of his computer screen throughout the day. He literally programmed himself to support the changes he wanted to make!

The "old tapes" you recorded by developing old habits are not erased by themselves. You erase them only by recording new tapes over the messages you no longer want to live by. Don't expect the new messages to last unless you replay them frequently.

Master the art of self-support.

The most crucial guideline for effective change is the need for continuing self support. If you have not developed and maintained a realistic self-confidence, then self-change will be difficult indeed. In Chapter 3 we highlighted the importance of catching yourself at being effective. It will not hurt to review that material here. We are not suggesting that you develop a swelled head; we are suggesting that you be aware of your strengths—at least as aware as you are of your mistakes. You may be changing and not realizing it because you focus only on those incidents that remind you of your old failures. Seek a balance that allows you to keep score of your effectiveness throughout the change process. Develop the habit of scanning yourself daily for evidence of your changes. Using the Post-it on your calendar can help to remind you to catch yourself being effective daily. By writing it down, you use it as a scorecard to give yourself evidence of your changes.

Don't limit your self-support to your calendar. Use staff meetings and one-on-one contacts at work to provide contexts for focusing on the

the neighborhood. Jerry Van Amerongen

9-23 Jerry VanAmerongen

Copyright 1986 Cowles Syndicate Inc.

Raymond puts a stop to his critical inner dialog.

positive. Instead of concentrating on the problems, take some time at meetings to ask, "What has been working lately?" At home, use the dinner hour to spread the idea of self-support to your spouse and children. Suggest that each member of the family report on what they did that day that made them feel positive about themselves; or what they learned from a mistake. All these strategies will help you and those you live and work with to begin to manage their own motivation.

There has to be room for mistakes along the road to change. Occasional slips and relapses into old habits are inevitable, and in the process of developing new ones we make many mistakes. Learn to rebound from your errors and your bad days by getting back into the challenge of changing. Accept each mistake as a setback that requires a recommitment to continued efforts to change. Avoid the tendency to wallow in self-doubt and self-deprecation. Instead, allow yourself to be motivated by your effectiveness and your recent successes.

Use self-contracts.

Don't just acknowledge your successes at self-change; take the time to reward yourself for them. Make a contract with yourself: "When I get to this point, I will have earned (some specified gift or activity)." Treat yourself: buy yourself something; take a walk or read a book; see a movie or play; call your high-school sweetheart, best friend, or mentor long distance. Too often we buy things for ourselves when we are depressed. We convince ourselves that it will make us feel better. Of course, it seldom works that way. Instead, we feel guilty. Reverse the process; treat yourself to something when you have earned it. You deserve it.

"Action is a great restorer and builder of confidence. Inaction is not only the result, but the cause, of fear. Perhaps the action you take will be successful; perhaps different action or adjustments will have to follow. But any action is better than no action at all. So don't wait for trouble to intimidate or paralyze you. Make a move."

—Norman Vincent Peale

Self-change is possible. By applying the guidelines introduced in this chapter, you can condition yourself successfully to any of the strategies and techniques we have presented in this book. You can become more adept at managing change and handling the conflict it creates; at deflecting or defusing problems before they become the cause of open warfare; at dealing with people assertively; at making change your ally in becoming a more effective leader. The choice is yours. You have some new tools; all that remains is for you to effect the changes. Best of luck— or rather, position, perform, and persist your way to better results.

"There is no such thing in anyone's life as an unimportant day."

—Alexander Woollcott

I'll leave you with one last story: a success story. The contents of this book represent an expansion of material I have developed and presented at my management seminars over the last several years. A mid-level manager at a Southern California video-production company was ordered by her boss to come to one of my seminars because of her abrasiveness. A year or so later, I attended a program sponsored by her company. She came up to me and introduced herself, reminding me that she had attended my seminar. Then she invited me up to her office to show me something she had there. It turned out to be a framed needlepoint that said—you guessed it—"BAGS TO JAPAN." She told me after I had shared that anecdote, she had not heard anything else I said. She spent her whole day thinking about where her luggage had gone and who had sent it. She used the needlepoint as a constant reminder of the number of times she had been right and nevertheless lost out because of her abrasive style. Every time anyone new saw it, she would retell the story. She never wanted to deal with people that way again. For a year she had worked with this reminder facing her desk, and during that year she had made significant changes in her ability to influence her workers, her peers, and her boss.

I laughed. I loved it. I'm ending this now to take up needlepoint.

QUESTIONS WORTH ASKING

"Do you have an answer for everything?"
No.

KEEPERS

☐ Focus your change efforts.

☐ Take change one step at a time to build on successes.

☐ Make commitments to build support.

☐ Use reminders to keep change on course.

☐ Catch yourself changing.

☐ Use self-reward to support changes, not setbacks.

☐ Skill retention is largely self-management.

REFERENCES

Bennis, Warren. *Why Leaders Can't Lead*. San Francisco, CA: Jossey-Bass, 1989.

Blanchard, Kenneth and Johnson, Spencer. *The One Minute Manager*. West Caldwell, NJ: William Morrow and Co., Inc., 1982.

Block, Peter. *The Empowered Manager*. San Diego, CA: University Associates, Inc., 1989.

Bolles, Richard Nelson. *The 1991 What Color Is Your Parachute?* Berkeley, CA: Ten Speed Press, 1991.

Byham, William C., and Cox, Jeff. *ZAPP! The Lightening of Empowerment*. San Diego, CA: University Associates, Inc., 1990.

Clance, Pauline Rose. *The Imposter Phenomenon*. Atlanta, GA: Peachtree Publishers, 1985.

Covey, Stephen R. *The 7 Habits of Highly Effective People*. New York: Simon and Schuster, 1989.

de Pree, Max. *Leadership Is an Art*. New York: Doubleday, 1989.

Fromm, Eric. *Man For Himself: An Inquiry into the Psychology of Ethics*. New York: Holt, Rinehart & Co., 1947.

Gardner, John W. *On Leadership*. New York: Free Press, 1989.

Geneen, Harold with Moscow, Alvin. *Managing*. New York: Doubleday & Co., Inc., 1984.

Greenleaf, Robert K. *Servant Leadership: A Journey into the Nature of Legitimate Power and Greatness*. New York: Paulist Press, 1977.

Harvey, Joan C., with Katz, Cynthia. *If I'm so Successful, Why Do I Feel Like a Fake? The Imposter Phenomenon*. New York: St. Martin's Press, 1984.

Hill, Norman C. *Increasing Managerial Effectiveness: Keys to Management and Motivation*. Reading, MA: Addison-Wesley Publishing Co., 1979.

Iacocca, Lee with Novak, William. *Iacocca: An Autobiography*. New York: Bantam Books, 1984.

Jamieson, David and O'Mara, Julie. *Managing Workforce 2000: Gaining the Diversity Advantage*. San Francisco, CA: Jossey-Bass, 1991.

Kanter, Rosabeth Moss. *The Change Masters*. New York: Simon and Schuster, 1983.

McClellend, D.C. and Burnham, D.H. "Good Guys Make Bum Bosses." *Psychology Today*, December 1975.

Miller, Lawrence M. *American Spirit: Vision of a New Corporate Culture*, New York: William Morrow & Co., Inc., 1984.

Newburger, Howard M. and Lee, Marjorie. *Winners and Losers*. New York: McKay, 1974.

Mooney, Richard L. "Performance Management—Staying on Top of the Job." A paper presented to the NACUBO National Convention, July 1976.

McNally, David. *Even Eagles Need a Push*. Eden Prairie, MN: TransForm Press, 1990.

Paulson, Terry L. *Making Humor Work*. Los Altos, CA: Crisp Publications, Inc., 1989.

Paulson, Terry L. *Management Dialogue*. Agoura Hills, CA: Paulson & Associates Inc., Quarterly Newsletter.

Paulson, Terry L. and Paulson, Sean D. *Secrets of Life Every Teen Needs to Know*. San Juan Capistrano, CA: Joy Publishing, 1990.

Peters, Thomas J., and Waterman, Robert H., Jr. *In Search of Excellence*. New York: Harper & Row Inc., 1983.

Phelps, Stanlee and Austin, Nancy. *The Assertive Woman: A New Look*. San Luis Obispo, CA: Impact Press, 1987.

Phillips, Steven L., and Elledge, Robin L. *The Team-Building Source Book*. San Diego, CA: University Associates Inc., 1990.

Rubin, David C. "The Subtle Deceiver: Recalling Our Past." *Psychology Today*, September 1985.

Tichy, N.M., and Devanna, M.A. *The Transformational Leader*. New York: John Wiley & Sons, 1986.

Toffler, Alvin. *The Third Wave*. New York: William Morrow and Co., 1980.

Tucker, Robert B. *Managing the Future: 10 Driving Forces of Change for the 90's*. New York: G. P. Putnam's Sons, 1991.

Vogt, Judith F., and Murrell, Kenneth L. *Empowerment in Organizations: How to Spark Exceptional Performance*. San Diego, CA: University Associates, Inc., 1990.

Waterman, Robert H. Jr. *The Renewal Factor*. New York: Bantam Books, Inc., 1987.